THE
GREEK AND ROMAN
WORLD

THE
GREEK AND ROMAN
WORLD

by W. G. HARDY

University of Alberta

Schenkman Books, Inc.
Rochester, Vermont

Copyright © 1970, 1991

Schenkman Books, Inc.
P.O. Box 119
Rochester, Vermont 05767

Library of Congress Cataloging in Publication Data
ISBN: 0-87073-111-4

CONTENTS

LIST OF PICTURES

THE GREEKS STEP ON STAGE

EVERY SCHOOLBOY KNOWS that the patterns set by the Greeks and Romans permeate our civilization; so much so that even our speech derives well over half its vocabulary from Latin and Greek. Politics, science, art, music, religion, athletics, philosophy—these are seven examples of English words which come from these so-called 'dead' languages. It is even more significant that the *ideas* those words express had their first connotations put into them by the Greeks and Romans.

Yet our legacy from each of these two great peoples is different. The Romans were the Marthas of Western civilization. The essence of our heritage from them is in practical things—engineering, for instance, and superior plumbing, as well as in a passion for order, discipline, law, and conformity; all of which are Latin words. The chief Greek contribution, however, is in art, literature, and ideas. It was the distinguished classicist, Mr. T. R. Glover, who once remarked: 'Rome is famed for its drains: Greece for its brains.'

Drains are useful and necessary. Yet in any appraisal of the value of Greece and Rome to the Western world, the gifts from the Greeks are the more important; and the Greeks, also, are the first of the two peoples to step into the limelight of history.

Who were these Greeks? Whence did they come? What was their geographical environment and how did it influence them? These seem to be questions which ought to be answered before we turn to how the Greeks lived, what they ate, how they were housed and, above all, how they looked at the world around them.

Until less than a century ago, it was thought that classical Greek civilization sprang almost full-fledged, from nothing. The *Iliad* and *Odyssey* of Homer, it is true, told about a great war of the Achaean Greeks against Troy about 1184 B.C. and of cities such as 'golden Mycenae' in Greece and 'wide-wayed Knossos' in Crete. But the epics of Homer, who is thought to have lived in the middle of the ninth century B.C., were regarded as mere legends, not as having something of history in them. Then, in 1870 A.D., the German businessman Schliemann found not one but nine cities on the hill of Troy. Of these, VII A, as it is called by archaeologists, is apparently the one destroyed by the Achaean Greeks. Six years later Schliemann went to the reputed site of 'golden Mycenae' in southern Greece. It was here, according to

FAYENCE SNAKE
GODDESS
MUSEUM, CANDIA
MIDDLE MINOAN

CUP BEARER
MUSEUM, CANDIA
LATE MINOAN

Homer, that Agamemnon, the leader of the Greeks against Troy, had ruled. And here Schliemann discovered, inside the outer wall, rock-cut, untouched tombs. From them he took golden cups, beautiful bronze daggers decorated with lions or birds in gold, and golden death-masks.

This find was enough to prove that there had been a high civilization in Greece from about 1700 B.C. on, centuries before the classical Greeks. Then in 1900 A.D., in search of the centre of this culture, the Englishman Sir Arthur Evans bought a small hill on the supposed site of 'wide-wayed Knossos' in Crete, sank a shaft, and struck stone. Today the remains of the six-acre palace of the Minos—the name of the ruler of Knossos—fascinate the tourist. Evans named this newly-discovered civilization, Minoan. It reached its peak from about 1600 to 1400 B.C. At Knossos the 'Queen's Rooms' were recovered almost intact. In the whole palace and the area around it—once a great city but now grain fields and olive orchards—were found jewels, bronze axes, copper cross-cut saws, marvellous fresco paintings of bulls and of men and women, a richly decorated gaming-board, and egg-shell-thin polychromatic pottery.

Since Evans and Schliemann, discovery has been piled on discovery. In Crete, other palaces such as the ones at Phaestos, Mallia, Hagia Triadha, and Kato Akro have been laid bare. In southern Greece Professor Blegen has excavated the great palace of Nestor at Pylos; at Mycenae, one of the most majestic sites anywhere, the Greek, George Mylonas, has unearthed another royal grave-circle. Here kings and queens of that far-off day were buried in gold-embroidered clothes, wearing gold diadems, gold breast-plates, and gold signet-rings. In one grave, a baby wrapped in gold foil was interred with its mother, and with the baby was buried a gold rattle. Homer's 'golden Mycenae' was fact, not fancy.

So, long before the Greeks of classical times, there had been a luxurious civilization which had centred in Crete and had spread northward into the Greek peninsula. The basic stock at first was the small, black-haired, olive-skinned Mediterranean race. There were broadheads, too, from Asia Minor. And then, shortly after 2000 B.C., big and predominantly blond intruders began to infiltrate northern Greece. At about the same time, incidentally, a similar people was pushing into North Italy, speaking a language akin to Latin.

In Greece these newcomers, although of differing tribes, were, in effect, the Achaeans. They came in small bands, driving their herds and flocks and bringing with them their ox-carts, their horses and rough chariots, and their wives and children—a

people in search of new homes. By 1700 B.C. they were in southern Greece. Here, like the Normans in Saxon England, they seem
to have established themselves as a ruling caste. Unlike the
Normans, they found, as we have seen, a higher culture—the
Minoan culture—in the land, and appropriated it. They traded
with the Minoans of Crete. They may have paid tribute to them.
Finally, apparently, about 1450 B.C., they attacked Crete and
overcame the Minoans. In their turn the Achaeans became the
dominant power in the Aegean Sea area, and their culture is
titled 'Mycenean' from their chief fortress-city at Mycenae.

These people, then, are 'the bronze-armoured Achaeans' of
whom Homer sings. They spoke an archaic form of Greek.
Their power endured for two centuries, from 1400 to 1200 B.C.
They had their splendid palaces and fortress-cities. They traded
with Egypt. They crossed the Aegean and settled in Asia Minor.
A street of Achaean merchants has even been found at the site
of Ras Shamra (ancient Ugarit) in Syria. They also went on
great raiding expeditions. In one of the last of these, about 1184
B.C., they captured and sacked Troy.

IVORY BULL-JUMPER
MUSEUM, CANDIA
LATE MINOAN

But, apparently, they had overextended themselves. At any
rate, in the twelfth century B.C., another Greek-speaking people,
the Dorians, took over in southern Greece, swept across Crete,
and reached Asia Minor. Many refugees from Greece also fled
across the Aegean to the coasts there, and settled north of the
Dorians.

The Dorians, like our own Anglo-Saxon ancestors, hated
cities. The rich Achaean fortresses were sacked. The Aegean
world slipped back into barbarism. Out of that dark night, about
the middle of the ninth century B.C., the classical Greeks began
to emerge. As you will realize, they were by this time a hodge-
podge of racial stocks. Basically, however, they were a fusion of
blond or brown-haired peoples from the north with the smaller,
darker-skinned Mediterraneans. In general they spoke some form
of one of the three major dialects of Greek—Aeolic, Ionic,
and Doric. They lived in small and primitive but intensely
patriotic city-states. Corinth, for example, possessed only 376
square miles of territory, and in the island of Crete there were no
less than forty-three separate city-states. Wars and feuds among
themselves were as frequent as between the Highland clans
of Scotland. Yet they all called themselves 'Hellenes' and
anyone who did not speak Greek was a *barbaros* from which
we have derived the word, 'barbarian'. This term was not at first
derogatory. It simply meant anyone using an incomprehensible

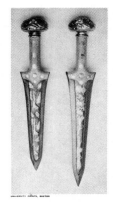

BRONZE DAGGERS
NATIONAL MUSEUM,
ATHENS
MYCENAEAN
C. 1570-1550 B.C.

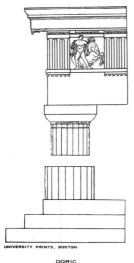

DORIC

IONIC

CORINTHIAN

language—a 'bar-bar' sort of person. Their homeland they named 'Hellas'. To them Hellas meant the Greek peninsula but not Macedonia, the islands of the Aegean, the coast of the eastward bulge of Asia Minor, and the Aegean Sea itself.

What was their homeland like? There is the sea first and foremost, Homer's 'wine-dark sea' of a deep, almost indigo blue, with at times a violet haze shimmering over it. There are the islands, stepping-stones to Asia. They and the harbours along the east coast of the Greek peninsula explain why Greece 'faces east' and why the classical Greeks were, after the Minoans, the first European people to come into contact with the ancient civilizations of the Nile and Mesopotamia. And then there are the mountains. From the sea or from the air Greece is ridge after ridge of tumbled peaks, smitten by the sun into russet or golden-brown or violet or purple.

The mountains and the sea present Greece with a sort of majestic beauty which surpasses the loveliness of Italy. But you cannot farm rocks. The Greek peninsula is only some 25,000 square miles in extent. It is smaller than Scotland, which has 29,280 square miles in it, and it is only a tenth the size of the province of Alberta. Yet of that 25,000 square miles, sixty-four-and-a-half per cent is bare stone. There are plains dropped down among the peaks and along the coasts like uneasy guests. All in all, however, only eighteen-and-a-half per cent of ancient Greece could be cultivated. Most of that small amount of soil is more fitted for barley, olives, and grapes than for wheat. Ancient Greece was, essentially, a goat and donkey country; while Italy means 'cattleland'.

The mountains had other major effects on the development of the Greeks. For one thing, they favoured the growth of small city-states, each separated from its neighbour; and the Greeks, of themselves, never achieved a nation-state. For another, it turned the people to the sea. To clamber up and down ridges is tough travelling; but no part of ancient Greece was more than fifty miles from the sea, and a boat swims easily to harbour. These harbours in the Greek world were countless, for the Mediterranean is a practically tideless sea. It was inevitable, then, that the Greeks, settled as they were on both sides of the Aegean as well as in the islands, should become mariners and traders. In summer, too, for most of the season, the Aegean is a glassy pond.

Greece is also a sub-tropical country. Even northern Greece lies south of Naples and some of you may know how hot Naples can become in June and July. At Athens in July, the daytime average maximum temperature, taken over a period of sixty-three years, is 98.71 degrees Fahrenheit in the shade, but the sand in the hot sun has been measured at 158 degrees. In January the average minimum temperature per day is a little over 33 degrees but the average maximum is 63. This means, for the men at least, an outdoor and socially gregarious life. 'Sub-tropical' also means a long dry season from the end of April to about the middle of September. Greek rivers can be raging torrents in autumn, winter, or spring. In summer their beds often become roads. A law-suit, in which the Greek orator Demosthenes took part, turned on a dispute as to whether a river-bed was a public highway, a water-course, or a private garden.

ELECTRUM EARRING FROM RHODES 7TH C. B.C.

To sum up, then, the homeland of the Greeks was a bare, rugged, and poor country. It had a compelling and austere beauty. By its very nature, however, it forced the people to develop fiercely independent city-states and to turn to the sea. Because, too, Greece, as has been noted, 'faces East', the Phoenician traders soon sought out the nascent Greek communities, bringing them goods and the alphabet, and giving them a push toward civilization. Inland from the Asia Minor Greeks, the country of Lydia, which was in touch with Mesopotamia, invented coinage and passed it on to the Greek cities. And then, about 750 B.C., a combination of circumstances set the Greeks hunting for new homes.

One cause was over-population, which is always a problem in a poor country. Another was the development of wealth and trade. This in turn sparked a struggle for political power between the old land-holding nobles and the newly-rich merchants. As in France or England later on, the side which lost often emigrated. Two famous Greek poets of Lesbos, Alcaeus and Sappho, were in exile for ten years because of faction fights. To these motives we must add the love of adventure. For from the eighth century B.C. to the sixth, the maritime cities of the Greek world were aboil with new ideas and new discoveries. As if to put the final spur to the surge outward of the Greeks, in the eighth century B.C. the Assyrians, the ruthless 'tigers of the East', con-quered the cities of Phoenicia.

This conquest interrupted the Phoenician control of the Mediterranean seaways. Into the vacancy swarmed the Greeks. It was an exciting period, these years when the Greeks sailed outward like flocks of birds seeking new nesting-places. Colonies from Chalkis and Eretria in the island of Euboea and from Corinth occupied the three-pronged promontory which thrusts out into the sea from Macedonia. Here the settlers were in

HERMES HOLDING A RAM 5TH C. B.C.

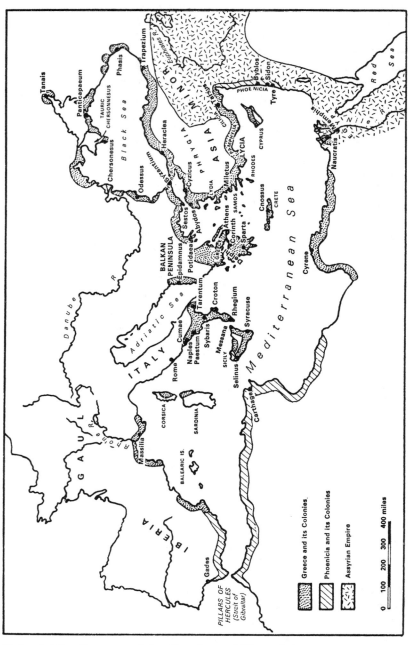

Colonial Settlements of the Greeks and Phoenicians

search of farmland, but were also looking for ship-timber, hides, and native ores. The Greeks put colonies along the Dardanelles, the Sea of Marmora, and the Bosphorus. The primary purpose was to control the passage into the Black Sea. One of these colonies, Byzantium, was to become Constantinople; today we call it Istanbul.

Greek sailors also burst into the Black Sea. They named it the Euxeinos, which means 'hospitable to strangers'. Land, the wheat of the Ukraine, fish, slaves, iron and silver—these were their objectives. There was also, as always, a huge profit to be made from trade with backward peoples. Miletus, one of the Greek cities of Asia Minor, is said to have planted ninety colonies around the Black Sea, chiefly for trade. For Miletus made and exported excellent textiles. Sinope, Trapezus, and Odessus are among their foundations, and the Crimea was dotted with settlements. Greek artifacts and something of Greek influence flowed up the rivers into Russia.

From Africa the Greeks were pushed away by the Egyptians and, further west, by the Carthaginians. Yet Miletus did secure a port at Naucratis on one of the mouths of the Nile. Thus, Egyptian linen, paper, and that peculiarly Egyptian animal, the cat, along with Egyptian knowledge, found their way to the Greek cities. Thales, the first Greek philosopher and the first Greek to predict an eclipse—the one of 28 May 585 B.C., was said to have studied in Egypt. Farther along the coast the little island of Thera put down a long-lasting colony at Cyrene in Libya.

The great Greek swarming, however, was westward. They faced difficulties. Carthage, originally a Phoenician colony, kept a jealous hold on the north shore of Africa and on the south-eastern and south-western coasts of Spain. Meanwhile, to the north, that mystery people, the Etruscans, were dominant in Italy and clung to Elba, Corsica, and Sardinia.

The Greeks were not to be denied. They dotted the heel, instep, and toe of Italy with their settlements. Northward they founded Cumae and Naples, for which their name was Neapolis, 'New City'. They took over the eastern part of Sicily. Syracuse, Naples, Messina, Girgenti, Taranto, Brindisi—these names all go back to the original Greek colonies. The settlers went still farther west. Modern Marseilles was ancient Greek Massalia. Through this port, by following the Rhône and Seine rivers, Greek traders appear to have reached England. Meanwhile so many colonies were established in Sicily and Italy that it was called 'Greater Greece'.

In these years, then, in search of land and trade, the curious, active Greeks took over the Black Sea and much of the Mediterranean area. A colony was usually decided upon by a meeting of those interested. After this, a common practice was to send to the oracle of Apollo at Delphi for information about where to go. Delphi, about 105 miles west of Athens, is set among majestic mountains on a ledge of Mount Parnassos. At this time it was one of the chief centres of Greek religion. We suspect that the priests of Apollo at Delphi must have maintained a good information centre. At any rate, as a rule they gave satisfactory advice. Incidentally, we know from the Greek philosphers, Plato and Aristotle, what the Greeks looked for in a site for a colony: first, tame natives, then good land, spring water, a harbour, a city-site not too near the sea for fear of pirates, and timber for ships.

Meanwhile, in the home city, an *oecist* or founder was appointed. When all was ready he took on board ship with him fire and a bit of soil from home. The rest of the emigrants—men, women, children, and animals—followed him. We can see and hear the frantic farewells, the looking back, and, perhaps, at the last moment, a man jumping to shore or a girl leaping on board. Then the tiny ship set out. When it reached the new home the *oecist* divided the land. He picked a place for a citadel. He apportioned the jobs in the new, strange country. He established the religious rites.

For from the moment the ship set sail the new colony was on its own. It had religious, commercial, and sentimental ties with its mother-city. Politically it was independent, not a colony at all in our sense of the term but a new slice of Greece. The word 'colony' is Latin and the Roman *colonia* remained under the control of its mother-city, Rome. But not the Greek colonies. There are cases of Greek colonies fighting against their home-city. Thus, in 435 B.C., Corcyra, now Corfu, defeated its mother-city, Corinth, in a great naval battle.

The obvious effects of this swarming outward of the Greeks were the relief of over-population at home and the increase of trade and wealth. The long-range results were more subtle. For one thing, each new colony became a centre which radiated outward the Greek way of life as a stove radiates heat. Romans and Etruscans, too, felt the influence. To give one example only, it was from the Greeks of Cumae that the Romans got the alphabet which they, in turn, passed along to us. Greek colonization was one factor which assured the impact of Greek culture on the Western world.

But ships are freighted with ideas as well as with goods. In

these centuries Greek horizons broadened. There was a burgeon-
ing of knowledge, the rise of a new and highly individualistic
poetry, and the beginnings of Greek philosophy.

All this was the expression of the changing era. But commerce also helped upset the economic balance in the home-cities—
commerce and the introduction of coinage and of interest, and of
the middle-man or retail trader. We have already seen how the
rise of the merchants led to struggles for power between them
and what we may call the 'squirearchy'—the aristocratic, land-
holding nobles. This latter class had, by the way, already, except
for Sparta, got rid of the kings.

Merchant versus land-holding aristocrat often led as at
Athens to a compromise between the two. They agreed to share
the government. But with coinage and retail trade and thriving
commerce, prices went up and up. The poor got poorer. Many
of the peasants were forced into debt-slavery.

An economic depression may easily have a dictator in its
pocket. Hence, in most of the maritime states of the Greek world
the economic crisis led to a tyranny. A Greek tyrant was, almost
always, a noble who, to quote Herodotus, 'took the people into
partnership'. He pretended to champion the cause of the poor,
got himself assigned a bodyguard, drove out or killed the other
nobles, and seized the power.

This story is as old as the Greeks and, *mutatis mutandis*, as
modern as this century. Often the tyrants ruled excellently. At
Corinth, Cypselus and his son Periander bettered the lot of the
poor, extended trade, and were patrons of art and literature. It
was Periander, Aristotle tells us, who when asked how he
prevented revolts took the questioner into a field of wheat. Periander did not say a word but, as he walked along, with his stick
he lopped off the tallest heads. Modern dictators have often
followed the same policy.

The tyrants, therefore, often served a useful purpose. Not
the least of these was that the second generation of them often
'disturbed ancestral custom, did violence to women, and killed
men without a trial'. As a result, the Greeks developed a passion
for freedom. When the tyrants were expelled, as they were in
most of the homeland states by 500 B.C., they were replaced
either by a government of the wealthy, called oligarchy, 'the rule
of the few', or, as at Athens, by a democracy, the rule of the
people.

No country, even in far-off times, can live to itself alone.
While the Greeks were colonizing and developing their city-

states, the Assyrian Empire had dissolved in a welter of blood. This had happened by 606 B.C. The second Babylonian Empire and the new Empire of the Medes and Persians, like the lion and the unicorn, contended for the crown. Meanwhile Lydia conquered the Greek cities of Asia Minor. They did not hold them for long. For Cyrus the Persian crossed the Halys River and defeated and captured Croesus, the last king of Lydia.

This was in 546 B.C. The Persians now took over the Asia Minor Greek states. They went on to capture Babylon and to conquer Egypt. Under Darius they crossed into Europe to subdue Thrace. When the Asia Minor Greeks revolted, and Athens and Eretria, a little city on the island of Euboea, sent twenty-two ships to help their brothers, the stage was set for the great struggle between the vast Persian Empire and the Greeks.

The odds seemed to be heavily weighted. The Persians had reconquered the Greeks of Asia Minor. Their empire stretched from central Asia and the frontiers of India to the first cataract of the Nile, and the Mediterranean Sea. They were reputed to be invincible. Many Greek states 'medized', that is, sent earth and water as symbols of submission to the great king, Darius.

There were two states, however, which spearheaded resistance. One was Dorian Sparta. Sparta was a country in which the individual was nothing and the state everything. But it did have the best fighting men in Greece. The other centre of resistance was Ionian and democratic Athens. As every history-book tells, when in 490 B.C. a large Persian army landed on the coast of Attica at Marathon, 9,000 Athenians and 1,000 Plataeans charged and broke it; 6,400 Persians were slain and 192 Athenians, less two who were removed in modern times, still sleep under the *soros* or mound which was put up over them where the fighting had been hottest.

PHOTO. THE ORIENTAL INSTITUTE, UNIVERSITY OF CHICAGO

DARIUS WITH CROWN PRINCE XERXES GIVING AN AUDIENCE TO A MEDIAN TREASURY, PERSEPOLIS
ACHAEMENIAN.   REIGN OF DARIUS.   491—485 B.C.

BRONZE ATHENA PROMACHOS STATUETTE
NATIONAL MUSEUM, ATHENS

ABOUT 500 B.C.

Marathon proved that the heavy-armed Greek *hoplite* could shear through light-armed Persians like a knife through butter. Herodotus added another explanation. 'Freemen,' he said, 'fight better than slaves.' In any case, the myth of Persian invincibility was shattered. Meanwhile Darius died. He was succeeded by his son Xerxes. In 480 B.C. Xerxes moved on Greece with a huge fleet and an army so immense that, to call on Herodotus once more, 'it drank the rivers dry'.

But in addition to the Greek army, there was now an Athenian fleet.

Every schoolboy also knows the final result. At Salamis, in 480 B.C., led by the Athenian squadron and Themistocles, the Greek fleet defeated the Persians. In the next year the Persian army was beaten at Plataea. In the same year as Salamis, the Western Greeks beat back the Carthaginians at Himera in Sicily. The Greeks in their fondness for the dramatic said that Himera and Salamis were fought on the same day.

The significance of the victories, however, is that the defeat of the Persians and Carthaginians was the torch to set fire to the brilliance of the great age of the Greeks. There was a tremendous upswelling of confidence. Like the English after the defeat of the Spanish Armada, the Greeks felt that there was nothing they could not attempt.

And nowhere more so than at Athens. When the dour Spartans withdrew from the Pan-Hellenic alliance, the Athenians formed the Ionian Confederacy of Delos. As its leaders they reopened the route to the Black Sea and freed the Greek cities of Asia Minor. Then, almost without at first knowing what they were doing, they turned the League into an Athenian Empire. They attacked Cyprus. They conquered a small land-empire. They invaded Egypt.

Alongside the commercial and political expansion marched a terrific development in art and literature. The great war with Sparta from 431 to 404 B.C. put a stop to Athenian political supremacy. But her cultural achievement continued and endured. It has been said, and with a good deal of truth, that in the fifth century B.C. 'the history of Athens is for us the history of Greece'.

In all too brief and insufficient a form, I have attempted to tell something about who the Greeks were and how they came to spread out around the Black Sea, and along the Mediterranean coasts. The political and economic changes which took place from the eighth to the close of the sixth century B.C. have been sketched, and the significance of the Persian Wars has been indicated. In the fifth century B.C. Athens towers above the Greek world. What made this tiny country great? How did its people live? What were their thoughts? These are the next obvious questions to face the student of the story of the Greeks.

2

LIFE IN FIFTH-CENTURY B.C. ATHENS (part one)

TODAY'S TRAVELLER to Athens almost inevitably climbs the flat-topped Acropolis. Around him are the ruined monuments of the fifth century before Christ—the Parthenon, the Erechtheum, the Propylaea or Entrance Gates, and the tiny but perfect Temple of Wingless Victory. Below him in sun-baked russet, pink, purple, and old rose is modern Athens.

To the north-east rises the bald-headed peak of Lykabettos. On three sides stretches, like a giant fish-hook, the Attic plain. Mountains hem in that plain. To the south-west, some four miles away, the Peiraeus, the harbour of Athens, thrusts out into the blue waters of the Saronic Gulf.

If, by some Wellsian time-machine, that traveller could be transported back into the fifth century B.C. the landscape and seascape would be much the same. Farmsteads, which according to the unknown author of the *Hellenica Oxyrhynchia* were the 'best furnished in Greece', would dot the Attic plain. The Aigaleos range and Pentelikos, from which the marble for the Parthenon came, and the long ridge of Hymettos, the honey mountain, would still shoulder into the blue sky. But the city beneath him would be much smaller. Modern Athens, along with the Peiraeus, houses more than a million people. The whole of ancient Attica had an estimated population of only from 270,000 to 300,000. Moreover, the streets below our traveller would be close-packed and great walls would enclose them. Two walls also ran in those days from Athens to the Peiraeus. These were 550 feet apart. A third wall thrust off to the roadstead of Phaleron, near which, today, the giant 'planes touch down. Into the space provided by those walls the population of ancient Attica crowded in time of war. For the power of Athens and the food for her people depended on control of the sea. In consequence, her great statesman, Pericles, had, in effect, made Athens into an island. Let the Spartan army march up if it wished; as long as the walls held and the Athenian war-fleet ruled the sea, Athens and her people could still survive.

It may be difficult for the modern North American, accustomed to vast distances and luxurious resources, to comprehend how small and how poor ancient Attica was. The word 'Attica' means a promontory. If one looks at a map of Greece one sees

ACROPOLIS FROM THE HILL OF THE MUSES. ATHENS

GREEK. GREAT BUILDINGS 447—409 B.C.

DRAWING BY RICHARD BOHN

THE ACROPOLIS OF ATHENS, RESTORED

GREEK. GREAT BUILDINGS 447—409 B.C.

why. Attica juts south-eastward into the Aegean Sea like a great wedge. The Cithaeron range cuts it off from the plains of Boeotia. The mountains of Megara hamper the invader who marches northward from the Isthmus of Corinth. The rest of Attica is protected by the sea and by the islands of Salamis and Euboea. As an added result the Athenians enjoyed the clearest air and the best climate in Greece. The Greek poet Pindar, often called the 'king of lyric poets', sang of 'violet-crowned Athens'.

But Attica, even if the island of Salamis is included, possesses only 886 square miles of territory, which is only a little larger than the area covered by London. Mountains sprawl over 386 square miles, or almost two-fifths of the country. In the plains the soil is thin. Ancient Attica grew chiefly vines, olive-trees, vegetables, fig-trees, and barley. There was plenty of stone for building, good clay for pottery, and silver at Laureion on the very tip of Attica. To feed her people, however, wheat and salt-fish had to be brought in from the Black Sea. It is not strange that in his famous *Funeral Speech*, delivered in the winter of 431–430 as a tribute to the Athenians killed in the first year of the Peloponnesian War, Pericles said: 'We love beauty with cheapness.'

UNIVERSITY PRINTS, BOSTON

RED-FIGURED
AMPHORA: THESEUS
CARRYING OFF
KORONE
ALTE PINAKOTHEK,
MUNICH
6TH C. B.C.

Yet in the fifth century B.C. this tiny and poor country, with a citizen body which never exceeded 43,000 adult Athenian males, won herself a small empire, and this in spite of the opposition of Corinth and Sparta.

This empire had only about three million souls in it. Yet it was, for the Greek world, a big one. There were ultimately, according to Sir Alfred Zimmern, about 250 communities, each bound to Athens by separate political and commercial treaties. The Aegean was an Athenian lake. Athenian warships guarded the entrance to the Black Sea and Athenian soldiers served in the islands, in Macedonia, and in Asia Minor. Fat-bellied merchantmen brought to the Piraeus linen and papyrus from Egypt, frankincense from Syria, dates and wheat flour from Phoenicia, pork and cheese from Syracuse, ivory from Africa, hides and cheeses from Gaul, woollens from Miletus, silver from Spain, iron ore from Elba, and the wheat of the Ukraine. 'The products of the world,' declared Pericles, 'flow into us.' Out from the Piraeus went Attic wines, shields and helmets and, above all, the famed Attic pottery.

In those years Athens swarmed with sculptors, painters, poets, historians, dramatists, architects, and philosophers. By 438 B.C. the Parthenon had been reared on her flat-topped Acropolis. In the theatre of Dionysus her citizens watched the tragedies of

EURIPIDES
MUSEUM, MANTUA

SOPHOCLES
LATERAN MUSEUM, ROME
C. 340 B.C.

SOCRATES
CAPITOLINE MUSEUM,
ROME
C. 325-300 B.C.

Aeschylus, Sophocles, and Euripides, and the comedies of Aristophanes. Pheidias, the master sculptor of all time, fashioned his famous Athene Parthenos of gold and ivory and those sculptures for the Parthenon, of which the best, as the Lord Elgin marbles, are now in the British Museum. Philosophers and rhetoricians such as Anaxagoras or Gorgias of Leontini or Socrates, the 'Great Agnostic', argued in her gymnasia and her streets. How one small city could reach such a height of intellectual, political, and artistic achievement at one and the same time, even if it were for only a half-century or so, remains a marvellous phenomenon.

These facts, and more, are necessary for our time-traveller to know if he is to understand the glittering temples around him on the Acropolis and the city beneath him. But in order to achieve a preliminary view of the way of life of fifth-century B.C. Athens, we may now turn to a leisurely day in the life of a fifth-century Athenian in May of the year 435 B.C. We will choose a middle-aged well-to-do citizen, with property in the country and an interest in his brother's trading ventures. His name will be Glaucon, son of Charicles.

On this morning, as on all mornings, Glaucon gets up at the crack of dawn, and for a very good reason. There are no electric lights. Instead, one has to depend on candles or on tiny wicks sputtering in clay or bronze lamps fed by olive-oil. With the type of lamps the Greeks had, one used as much daylight as one could. When, for example, Hippocrates wanted to take Socrates to visit the Sophist or 'Wise Man', Protagoras, he arrived before dawn and 'gave a terrific thump on the door with his stick'. Socrates let him in. Hippocrates was all a-twitter to start out immediately.

'Not yet, my good fellow,' said Socrates. 'Let us take a turn in the court and wait until about daybreak. When the day comes, then we will go.'

Thus, our Athenian, Glaucon, is up before the sun rises. After washing, he puts on his tunic, which is a sleeveless garment, and has his breakfast. This is merely a bit of bread dipped in wine. Meanwhile, his women-folk will be drawing water and beginning to clean up in preparation, possibly, for a day at the loom. The house in which they move about is at best a flimsy structure. Public buildings in Athens glittered in marble. Private dwellings were built of sun-dried brick. It is no accident that the Greek word for burglar meant 'a man who digs through walls' When, for instance, in the Peloponnesian War, the Thebans occupied Plataea by a sudden night incursion and the Plataeans decided to attack them, the Plataeans got together secretly by digging through the walls of their houses; and all this, occupation and counter-attack, took place in a single night. Houses, too, faced inward upon one or more central courts. Except for the door, there was a blank wall toward the street. Many homes, however, had a second storey. Here, there were usually two or three narrow and glassless windows. On the ground floor, among other rooms, there was one particularly large room which usually did double duty as a dining-room and work-room.

At the back were the women's quarters, or else these could be upstairs. In Dorian Sparta women had a good deal of freedom. In Ionian Athens respectable women were kept in semi-Oriental seclusion. Boys got formal schooling. Girls were trained at home in the domestic arts. When the time for marriage came it was arranged for by the parents. The bride was usually fifteen, while her husband would be at least thirty. After marriage the woman's duty was to bear children and to manage the household. She could go calling and attend the festivals and tragedies, but not comedies. But she was supposed to say little and not to be seen. In his funeral speech Pericles' advice to women was that 'the best among you is she who is least spoken of among men for good or ill'.

PERICLES
VATICAN, ROME
C. 440 B.C.

There was a class of women who mingled freely with men. These were the *hetairai* or companions. They were highly educated in music, poetry, and dancing, and their status was apparently much like that of the Japanese geisha. The Athenian matron may at times have envied them. We can feel certain, though, that the influence of Athenian women on their men was considerable. For example, Themistocles, the great Athenian statesman, once said, 'I rule Athens and Athens rules Greece and my wife rules me and the child rules her.' And that is a statement which sounds remarkably familiar.

Yet the lives of women were, on the whole, quite restricted. Athens was a man's city. Women spent much of their time in simply furnished houses which were hot in summer and cold and draughty in winter. Their husbands lived most of their waking hours out of doors.

MAIDEN (CARYATID)
BRITISH MUSEUM,
LONDON
C. 421-409 B.C.

And so, on this May morning of 435 B.C., our Athenian Glaucon prepares for the street by putting on his *himation*. This is a wrap-around, usually of wool and usually white. The cavalry men or knights, and young bloods in general, often replaced the *himation* by a *chlamys* or cloak in bright colours—scarlet or frog-green or purple. A farmer normally wore only his tunic at work, and this so arranged as to leave the right arm and shoulder bare. Artisans, such as the potters or iron-workers, made do with a leather apron. But a well-to-do Athenian such as Glaucon regularly put on a *himation* and paid careful attention to the way its folds hung. Its length is supposed to reach the lower part of his shins. For his feet he has a choice between sandals or boots or he may even, like Socrates, walk about barefooted. On his head he wears nothing but his hair. It and his beard are always carefully trimmed and oiled. If Glaucon were going to the country where, we will presume, he owns a farm, he might indulge himself with a broad-brimmed hat called a *petasos*. In the city, a hat would be out of place.

His only adornment is a signet-ring, though he does carry a walking-stick. Thus dressed, Glaucon goes past the porter whose post is in the vestibule. Two slaves follow him into the street. The number of slaves in fifth-century B.C. Attica is variously estimated at from 80,000 to 150,000; 90,000 is probably a fairly sound figure. Since the number of Athenians, men, women and children, ranges from 120,000 to 170,000 and the total number of *metics* or resident aliens is generally reckoned at about 45,000, it is evident that slaves are a very important element in the population. Slavery, naturally, is taken for granted by both slaves and masters in every country of the civilized world of the day.

We must not, however, think of Athenian slavery in terms of Harriet Beecher Stowe's *Uncle Tom's Cabin*. For one thing, there was no colour distinction. For another, some of the slaves in the Greek world were Greeks. Many of them, of course, were foreigners—barbarians from Thrace or the Black Sea area, Gauls, Syrians, and the like. The fact is, moreover, that if Glaucon were captured in battle, he might very well be sold into slavery. This was the fate which befell the survivors of the Athenian army after the defeat of the Sicilian expedition of 415-413 B.C.

Slavery, then, was something which could happen to anyone. In that statement, perhaps, lies the key to the kindly treatment of slaves in ancient Athens. Moreover, slaves could often find refuge in a neighbouring country. In the last phase of the Peloponnesian War of 431-404 B.C., 20,000 Athenian slaves are said to have deserted to the Spartans.

At any rate, contemporary Greek authors give us evidence that Athenian slaves were the best treated in Greece. If they were hired out for wages by their masters, they worked side by side with free men and received the same pay, a fact which is proved by the Erectheum inscriptions of 409 B.C. They were sometimes set up in a shop. In both cases slaves were allowed to keep part of their earnings and were permitted to buy their freedom.

It is true that in lawsuits, each side regularly offered its slaves for torture to prove the truth of their allegations. We may suspect that this was, pretty largely, a legal manoeuvre. It is known that a slave could not, as was the case in Rome, be put to death at the whim of his master. Only his master could chastise him and this right appears to have been limited by law to fifty strokes, though fifty seems quite enough. Furthermore, an Athenian slave could flee to sanctuary from a cruel master and demand to be sold to someone else. For a final proof of the general treatment of slaves in Athens, we

UNIVERSITY PRINTS, BOSTON

SCYTHIAN SLAVE SHARPENING KNIFE ("KNIFE-GRINDER")
UFFIZI, FLORENCE
ABOUT 240—200 B.C., ROMAN COPY

may turn to a contemporary document written by an Athenian, name unknown, who was highly critical of Periclean democracy. Hence, he is usually called 'the Old Oligarch'.

'At Athens,' says the Old Oligarch, 'the impudence of slaves . . . is at its peak. To strike them is not permitted there, and yet a slave will not stand out of the way to let you pass. For . . . if it were lawful for a slave to be struck by a free man . . . you would often think an Athenian a slave and hit him.'

From this statement about slavery, the slaves in the silver mines at Laureion must be excepted. These mines were let out to contractors for a fixed price. To make profits, the contractors worked their slaves in narrow galleries under deplorable living conditions. Only the very toughest survived. With this qualification, slavery in Athens was as humane as it is ever likely to be. It should be emphasized, too, that though slaves were, as the philosopher Aristotle termed them, 'living implements', free men as well as slaves did manual work in Athens. Ancient Greek economy did not rest wholly on a slave base. It was also a fifth-century B.C. Greek Sophist who was the first man of whom we know to protest against slavery as unjust and unnatural.

Glaucon, our Athenian, has been left standing outside his home for some little time. His objective, as he moves off, is the Agora or market-place. The street down which he walks is narrow and twisting, and made still narrower by projecting balconies. There is dust blowing and offal lying about. Up front, a pot of slops is emptied from an upper window. For there is no sewerage-system in Athens, and no garbage-collection either.

Glaucon's nose is, naturally, used to it. As he comes to a corner he falls in with a friend. As they glance up, there is a quick glimpse of the gleaming temples on the Acropolis. At its north-western corner, the bronze statue of Athene Promachos, fifty feet high, thrusts a spear up into the blue sky. When the two men, followed by their slaves, enter the Agora, to their right and above them is the Hephaesteion, today usually called the Theseum—a splendid example, second only to the Parthenon, of Doric architecture. On their own level and to their right are some of the public buildings of the city. Notable among them is the council chamber—the Bouleuterion. In it a group of the Councillors of Athens are always on duty. Next door are kept the official weights and measures of the city, some of which can be seen today in the museum housed in the lately-rebuilt Stoa of Attalos.

Around the two men are temples, shrines, porticoes, colonnades, and swarms of men. Every male resident of Athens who has any leisure time at all regularly pays a morning visit to the Agora. In the Agora one hears all the rumour and gossip of the day—the story of the trouble between Corinth and its colony, Corcyca, which was to lead to a major naval engagement and an

UNIVERSITY PRINTS, BOSTON

PARTHENON FROM THE NORTHWEST, ATHENS
GREEK. 447—432 B.C.

alliance between Corcyca and Athens; the current price of wheat; the latest witticism at the salon of Aspasia, Pericles' common-law wife; predictions of what the Spartans or Persians are likely to do; discussions about the most recent law-suit or about the next resolution to be introduced to the Assembly—everything which is floating in the air of Athens finds its way to the Agora.

Glaucon finally makes his way to that part of the Agora which is used as a market. Here everything is in sections—stalls for fruits, vegetables, fish, flowers, pots, and so on, each in their own division. There is a tangled crowd surging around the stalls, chiefly men. In ancient Athens the men do the buying and the only free-women to be seen are those of the poorer class. Notable among these are the bread-women, who are famed for their coarse but effective repartee. There are, however, market commissioners to keep order. They have market police at their call. It might be noted that the police of ancient Athens were Scythian slaves, armed with bows. We will assume that Glaucon is giving a dinner this evening for his brother, who has just returned from a voyage to Miletus. Consequently, he will be buying fish, bread, vegetables, fruit, and the like. He hires a chef, too. In ancient Athens, one's women-folk are not trusted to cook an important meal. The best cooks are those who have been trained in Syracuse, and a Syracusan chef in those days carried the same cachet as a Parisian chef does today. There is also a section of the market in which acrobatic dancers and other entertainers can be secured. Since he is giving only a modest dinner, Glaucon contents himself with a couple of flute-girls.

THE "THESEUM" (TEMPLE OF HÉPHAESTUS AND ATHENA). ATHENS
GREEK. 450—440 B.C.

UNIVERSITY PRINTS, BOSTON

OLD MARKET WOMAN
METROPOLITAN MUSEUM OF
ART, NEW YORK
2ND C. B.C.

All this is carried out to the accompaniment of a great deal of bargaining about quality and price, in which the slaves are apt to join. For there is a true social democracy in ancient Athens; besides, haggling is half the fun of marketing.

Once the buying is done, Glaucon will turn over his purchases to his slaves and, in all probability, pay a visit to his banker. In ancient Athens instead of the question, 'What bank do you use?' one asks, 'At what table do you deal?' The word for banker means, in fact, 'a tableman'. Each banker brings his table with him, sets it up in the part of the market reserved for bankers, arranges his piles of coins on it, and is open for business. Much of the banking business has to do with the changing of coinage, since each little city-state mints its own silver and copper coins, and these are of different weights and of differing purity. By the Periclean period, however, letters of credit and loans at interest are in vogue. So Glaucon has in mind, we will suppose, an advance against the returns from his farm in order to invest in a cargo of wheat to be imported from the Black Sea area.

By this time, it is what the Athenians called 'full market', that is, about ten o'clock. Time is told chiefly by public sun-dials. Invitations for dinner, for instance, were often issued for 'when the shadow is ten feet, or twelve feet'. Some houses, however, kept an hour-glass-shaped pot; but water, not sand, was used. When his business is finished, Glaucon will inevitably drift over to his favourite barbershop. Barbershops, along with chemists' shops and doctors' offices, abound in the streets around the Agora. Here one gets a beard- and hair-trim and also meets one's friends. There is more talk followed by a stroll along one of the colonnades. Politics is certain to be hotly discussed. There are no true political parties in our sense of the term, except for a general division into Oligarchs, or conservatives, versus Democrats. Rather, each special group has its spokesman. What is today termed by historians 'the Peiraeus-party' of rich merchants is likely to support Pericles. But each good speaker in the Assembly has his coterie of partisans. Each citizen is likely to be keenly interested. For, as we shall see, the Assembly of its male citizens rules Athens and the empire. Consequently, politics is of absorbing everyday interest to the Athenians.

When it is time for luncheon Glaucon goes home. Lunch is a substantial meal, taken with his wife, two sons, and a daughter. After luncheon, Glaucon will rest and, possibly, read part of a play or a philosophical work. Then, like all his friends, he will set out for one of the three gymnasia which stand outside the gates in the suburbs of Athens.

DISCOBOLOS (DISCUS THROWER)
VATICAN, ROME

AFTER MYRON, c. 460—450 B.C., ROMAN COPY

These gymnasia—the Academy, Lyceum, and Cynosarges—are, in effect, men's clubs. Only freemen over eighteen can enter. There are rows of plane-trees, terraces, benches, and open spaces for exercise. Middle-aged men, such as Glaucon, will content themselves with a game of catch or some form of mild exercise. The younger men, however, will be violently engaged in wrestling, running, boxing, throwing the javelin or the discus, broad jumping, and the like. Athletics were a regular feature of Greek life and everyone was supposed to participate.

But there were also rooms for games and for lectures. In the fourth century, for example, the great philosopher Plato lectured at the Academy. Over the entrance to his room was written, we are told: 'Let no one enter here who does not know geometry.'

The gymnasium, then, is an outstanding feature of Athenian

life. Glaucon will talk, exercise, have a bath, and talk some more. Greek baths, incidentally, were not the elaborate establishments which the Romans later developed. In Greek bathing one washed piecemeal from a sort of vat on a stand and then had the bathman pour water over one. For soap there was only a mixture of wood-ashes and a special kind of clay or fullers' earth or, of course, olive-oil. The *strigil*, that curved sort of instrument seen in the statue called the Apoxyomenos, was used to scrape the dirt off the skin.

When Glaucon reaches his home again, the couches will have been pulled out and dinner will be ready. The women-folk will have retired to their own part of the house. A formal dinner is for males only. When the guests arrive, they will recline on the couches, the three-legged tables will be pulled out, and the food served. There are no knives or forks. Fingers are used and occasionally a spoon.

The meal itself is simple. Eels are a delicacy but fish is more likely to be the main course. Along with it will be served vegetable dishes drenched with olive-oil or honey or with sauces of varying sorts, and bread. Soft bread will be used to wipe off the fingers. This, along with other debris, will be flung to the dogs or on the floor.

After the first course, hands are washed, the floor swept, a chant sung to the accompaniment of music from the flute-girls, a libation to good health poured, and the second tables, or dessert, brought in. This, too, is not elaborate. It consists of fruit, chiefly figs and apples, almonds, cakes, cheese, and salt. Salt, by the way, is expensive and a frugal Athenian was described as 'one who burrows with his thumb in his salt-cellar'.

When the meal is done the symposium begins. The word means 'drinking together'. The average Athenian, however, is temperate. He never drinks unmixed wine. Usually water and wine are mingled in the proportions of three of water to two of wine. The chief purpose of drinking is to keep a conversation going. There may be a discussion of trading prospects in Asia Minor. The talk is more likely to turn again to politics or to literary or artistic criticism or to philosophy, as in that dialogue of Plato which is titled *Symposium*. Even in the fifth century B.C., however, professional diners-out, called 'shadows', with a repertoire of jokes and stories, were to be found. If anyone did overdrink, he would be called 'wet' or 'dipped' or 'chest-protected'. The comic poet Aristophanes, however, gives the view of the average Athenian. 'Drinking is bad,' says Aristophanes, 'for wine means banging at doors, hitting people and having to pay for it, and a headache into the bargain.'

When Glaucon's symposium is over, the slaves guide their masters home through the unlit streets with torches or horn-lanterns. Then, at last, Glaucon makes ready for bed.

It may be fairly urged that this sketch of a day in the life of an average, middle-aged, well-to-do Athenian is too lazy a day. It is quite true that there would be occasions when Glaucon would have much more business to occupy him. In war-time, too, he would be likely to be serving in either the army or the navy; while in peace-time, at some period in his life, he would in all probability be selected by the lot as a magistrate or councillor to give full-time duty to the state. There might also be times when he would have a law-suit on his hands.

Yet even the poor took more leisure time than we. Life, the ancient Athenians seem to have believed, was meant for living rather than for a mad scramble in search of possessions.

The poor, however, had to work harder than the well-to-do. Their food was also more monotonous. Apart from vegetables and fruits in season, the staple dish was barley-porridge or barley-cakes with a bit of salt-fish or an onion as a relish. On festival days, there might be a piece of kid or lamb or veal. Blood-puddings, tripe, and sausages were popular. Aristophanes, in one of his plays, with a touch of modernity, accuses the butchers of making sausages out of dog or donkey meat.

There were not too many gay young bloods in ancient Athens. Food in their case was more varied. For amusement they could train race-horses, as Alcibiades, the nephew of Pericles, did, or hold cock-fights, or participate in joint-contribution dinners, or keep an expensive courtesan. There were, however, few social barriers—that is, if a man possessed intellect. Socrates, the stonemason, was welcome at the tables of the wealthy; and even the gay Alcibiades is represented in Plato's *Symposium* as abandoning the wine-cup for a philosophical discussion.

Ancient Athens lacked much which to us is commonplace. Yet there does seem to have been an active life of the mind and the body, at least for the men. There were the gymnasia. There were the athletics festivals, which were also religious in character. Religious, too, were the torch-races and the two annual dramatic festivals in which European drama was born. Above all, perhaps, was the consciousness in the minds of its citizens that Athens was not only an imperial city but also the artistic and cultural centre of the Greek world. 'We are a school to Hellas,' Pericles proclaimed. In these words he seems to have captured the pride of Athenians in their city.

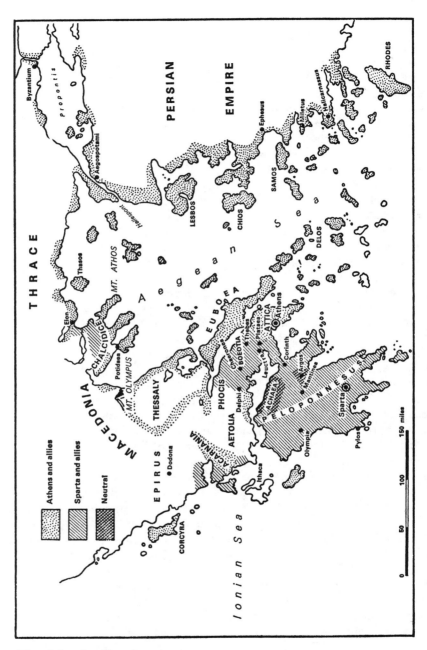

The Athenian Empire

3

LIFE IN FIFTH-CENTURY B.C. ATHENS (part two)

FROM 445 TO 431 B.C. Athens was, more or less, at peace. Yet every citizen knew that to the south frowned Corinth, the trade-rival of Athens, and that, behind Corinth, dour and jealous Sparta was waiting for a chance to pounce.

In 431 B.C., to change the metaphor, the storm-cloud burst and the Peloponnesian War began. It lasted, in three separate phases, for twenty-seven years. Athenian sea-power was matched against Spartan land-power. Finally, in 404 B.C., Athens lost the war. One reason for her defeat was the Great Plague of 430-429 B.C. That plague is described in detail by a man who lived through it, the Athenian general and historian Thucydides. It seems to have been the same Black Death or bubonic plague which was, later, to scourge medieval Europe. This catastrophe carried off at least one-fourth of the population of Attica. 'The bodies of dying men lay one upon another,' wrote Thucydides.

To that plague succumbed Athens' greatest statesman, Pericles, along with two of his sons. After his death the war continued for 25 years under lesser men, such as Cleon the tanner, who gained control of the Athenian democracy. In 421 B.C., after Cleon had been killed in battle, the Peace of Nicias, which left both sides just as they had been, was negotiated. If Athens had been content with that peace, she might have held her empire. But now Alcibiades, the brilliant nephew of Pericles, came to the fore. At his persuasion, in 415 B.C., Athens sent out a great armada to conquer Syracuse and Sicily. It left the Peiraeus in bright sunshine, and the captains, Thucydides tells us, raced their ships for fifteen miles as far as the island of Aegina. The whole force of Athenians and their dependent allies numbered finally 134 *triremes*, the warships of the day. These *triremes* carried altogether some 30,000 soldiers, of whom 5,100 were *hoplites*, the heavy-armed infantry who were the backbone of a Greek army. Along with that fleet sailed a mob of merchants in smaller craft, as if to a giant fair.

Neither that armada which set out so gaily, nor the reinforcements dispatched to it, were to return. Two years later its miserable survivors were sold in the slave markets of Syracuse. Athens lost 240 warships and some 40,000 men from her own citizens and from her subject allies. And now the Spartans renewed the war.

When it is remembered that, apart from her subject states, Athens started the war with not more than 43,000 citizens and about 10,000 *metics*, or resident aliens, of fighting age, it seems clear that any lesser city would have collapsed. Athens fought on. Then Persian gold bought Sparta a fleet. The subjects of Athens, who had been held in check by Athenian sea-power, were at last able to revolt. In 405 B.C. the last Athenian war-fleet was captured at Aegospotamoi and 4,000 prisoners-of-war were butchered like helpless cattle. The Spartan army marched to the walls of Athens. The Spartan fleet blockaded her harbour, the Peiraeus. Athens had always had to import the greater part of her food. In April of the next year the city was starved into surrender. Democratic imperialism had failed. The great age was over.

Yet in the long agony of war, as in the golden but too brief years of peace, the Assembly of the Athenians, except for a few short months, continued to govern. The Temple of Wingless Victory and the Erechtheum, both of them graceful achievements in the Ionic order of architecture, were completed. Citizens and *metics* still crowded the theatre of Dionysus to applaud or hiss the plays of Sophocles, Euripides, Aristophanes, and their compeers.

How could the Athenians have held out so long? Why were they so in love with their city that they were willing, in Pericles' words, 'to give their bodies to the commonwealth . . . and adjudging happiness to be freedom and freedom, courage, not idly to stand aside from the enemy's onslaught'?

Part of the answer lies in Pericles' own words. In Athenian democracy, 'liberty' was not a mouthed word, but actuality. Another reason is to be found in Athenian values. They had many faults. But, to paraphrase Goethe's words, they seem to have dreamed the dream of life well. To understand them, let us consider how an Athenian was reared and what occupied him when he became an adult.

First of all, by way of contrast, consider Sparta. Here the state determined what children were to live. The sickly and deformed were exposed on the slopes of Mount Taygetus; the rest got a military education. Sparta was a warrior state.

In Athens, as in most Greek cities, the decision as to whether a child was to be accepted or not was left to the father. If he was poor and had too many children, it was within his rights to refuse the infant. In that case the baby was put in an earthen-ware jar and exposed near a temple in the hope that some passerby might take pity on it. An amulet or trinket was left with the child, and we can well imagine the mother watching tearfully from nearby to see what the fate of her baby would be. Girl-children were more often exposed than boys.

The prevalence of this abhorrent custom is proved, among other references, by those plots of Greek New Comedy which turn on the recognition of such an exposed child through the tokens left with it. Yet no people were fonder of children than the ancient Greeks. The apparent contradiction is to be explained by the poverty of the Greek world. Infanticide was their answer to over-population.

In fifth-century B.C. Athens, with prosperity perched on her ships, infanticide seems to have been infrequent. Sons, in particular, were eagerly welcomed. For the first seven years boys and girls were brought up together in the women's quarters. There were plenty of toys—rattles, balls, hoops, swings, toy carts and wagons, tops, and dolls with movable limbs. Small dogs, tortoises, and ducks were among the pets. There were no cats. The family mouser was either a weasel or a pet snake.

At about the age of seven, however, girls began to learn domestic duties, while boys were assigned a *paidagogos* and sent to school. The *paidagogos* from which our word 'pedagogue' is derived, was not a teacher. He was a slave and his task was to supervise every waking moment of the boy's life.

NIOBE AND DAUGHTER
UFFIZI, FLORENCE
C. 320-280 B.C.

All Athenian schools were private schools, with the father paying fees at the end of each month. There was no compulsory education either, but public opinion was such that practically all Athenian boys attended school from the age of seven to the age of fourteen. Almost every Athenian man could write, though few women could. The curriculum, limited to boys only, was not vocational. Its objective was to teach the boy 'the three r's' and to produce 'a sound mind in a healthy body'. Writing was taught by helping the pupils shape the letters and then practise them, along with phrases and sentences, on a wooden tablet smeared with wax. In this wax the child wrote with a stylus made of bone, ivory, or metal. In shape the stylus was like an exaggerated toothpick with a pointed end for writing and a blunt end for erasures. Not until the Greek youngster could write well was he allowed to use ink and a reed pen on papyrus, the ancient world's anticipation of our paper.

Reading, naturally, went hand in hand with writing. The Athenian boy learned his alphabet, proceeded to simple phrases and sentences, and then read and memorized in whole or in part Homer's great epics, the *Iliad* and the *Odyssey*. Memorization was supposed to train the mind, while the nobility of the characters and motivations in Homer were believed to shape the youngster's character. We read in Xenophon, the fourth-century B.C. Athenian educationist, economist, and historian, of a man who could still recite from memory all of the *Iliad* and the *Odyssey*—close to 28,000 lines of poetry. Such a feat was, apparently, not uncommon.

The other elementary subject, arithmetic, was difficult to handle. Like we ourselves, until we imported Arabic numerals, the Greeks had no sign for zero, while their numbers were letters of the Greek alphabet with arbitrary values assigned to them. To comprehend the difficulty, we must, if we are capable of so doing, put zero and Arabic numerals out of our minds and multiply, add, and subtract with Roman numerals only.

Both the Greeks and the Romans solved this difficulty by the use of the *abacus,* which was first employed in ancient Egypt. In this, rows of counters were moved this way and that, the top line representing units, the second tens, the third hundreds, and so on.

The more advanced curriculum was divided into music and gymnastics. The Greek term *mousike* included poetry. Consequently, the student now added to Homer, Hesiod, the didactic poet, and the writers of elegiac, iambic, and lyric verse. He was also taught to play the lyre and to sing to it, and at times

UNIVERSITY PRINTS, BOSTON

WRESTLERS
UFFIZI, FLORENCE
SCHOOL OF PERGAMON, ABOUT 240—200 B.C., ROMAN COPY

BLACKSMITH'S SHOP
AMPHORA. LATE BLACK-FIGURED STYLE

instruction in the flute was added. Greek vase-paintings occasion-ally depicted school scenes. In one of these a teacher and a pupil are seated, both with lyres, while the teacher shows the boy where to place his fingers. Music was supposed to produce a harmonious character. Physical education, however, was regarded as of almost equal importance. Boys were taught wrestling, swimming, danc-ing, throwing the discus and javelin, and running and jumping, but not boxing or the *pankration,* which was a sort of all-out wrestling. Incidentally, there was no nonsense about sparing the rod. Athenian children went to school before sunrise knowing that the stick and strap were waiting.

In this way a boy was given what we would call a liberal education until fourteen or, in some cases, until sixteen. Home training was not neglected. Boys had to stand when their elders were present and were not to speak until spoken to.

When his schooling was done, the youth learned his voca-tion. He might enter his father's shop to become a potter. Or he might be taught how to manage his father's property, or work on the family farm. Meanwhile, his education continued inform-ally. He listened to the political, artistic, and philosophical dis-cussions of his elders. He attended the religious festivals. He went on with his athletics. Each year at Athens there were the games at the Panathenaea; and the best of the young men would train for the great games, such as the Olympic games. Then, at

UNIVERSITY PRINTS, BOSTON

DIONYSUS IN A BOAT. INTERIOR
OF ATTIC BLACK-FIGURED KYLIX
STAATLICHE ANTIKENSAMMLUNGEN, MUNICH
GREEK. VASE PAINTING BY EXEKIAS.
c. 540 B.C.

MUSEUM OF FINE ARTS, BOSTON

AMPHORA ATTRIBUTED TO THE
ANDOKIDES PAINTER

the age of eighteen, the Athenian young men became citizens and entered the army for two years. They took an oath, which is quoted in the *Florilegium* of Stobaeus, not to desert their comrades, to defend the constitution, to respect the laws and the religious practices, and to leave their fatherland 'greater and better' than they had received it. During the first army year they served in Attica. In the second they were sent out for duty throughout the empire. When they returned, it was with some idea of the greatness of their city.

This was the 'old-time education'. From about 450 B.C., however, those who could afford it could take a sort of university curriculum from the Sophists. The word meant 'Wise Men'. The Sophists clustered to Athens. They taught geometry, astronomy, ethics, politics, grammar, literature, and the like. Their fees were high. From the *Apology* of Socrates we learn that the Sophist, Evenus, charged five *minai*, or about $2,000, a course. Above all they taught people to speak. For in democratic Athens ability to speak was a key to success. The comic poet, Aristophanes, accused the Sophists of atheism and of 'making the worse appear the better reason'.

These were natural accusations against teachers who fostered free inquiry and scepticism. Around the Sophists centred much of the exciting intellectual ferment of Periclean Athens. Yet people must eat and sleep as well as think and talk. It is time, perhaps, to take a look at workaday Athens.

Until the Peloponnesian War, many Athenians were still on the farm and many city-dwellers held property in the country. The main character of the *Clouds,* in which Aristophanes made an attack on Socrates and the new education, is Strepsiades, a farmer. He is represented as old-fashioned and stupidly cunning but by the end of the play he has become the common-sense backbone of the state.

Yet Periclean Athens was, after all, one of the major trading-centres of the Mediterranean. This pre-eminence was won and maintained by bankers, wholesale traders, and merchant-skippers, but above all by her craftsmen.

Today, north of the Acropolis, there is a narrow street called Shoe Lane. If you walk down it, on both sides of you are shoes and boots and still more boots and shoes. Shoe Lane is a sort of vestigial reminder of industry in ancient Athens. There were shoemakers, metal-workers, dyers, tanners, jewellers, stonemasons, and a host of other craftsmen. But instead of mass-production in huge factories crammed with machinery, Athenian shoes, pots, sausages, hoes, axes, and the like were turned out by workers in small shops. These shops were often both the plants for manufacturing the goods, and the outlets for selling them. Often, as in much of the Near East today, they were also the homes of the craftsmen. Most of these small plants were run by a man and his apprentices, aided by a slave or two. To make the situation still more confusing from a North American point of view, all the workers of one craft lived side by side. The potters of Athens, for instance, all crowded together in the Cerameicus; just as in Cicero's first *Catilinarian* there is a reference to the 'Street of the Scythe-Makers'.

ATHENA POURING WINE
FOR HERCULES
MUNICH
C. 480 B.C.

If you will allow your imagination to roam for a moment, you can hear the hammers of the sweating metal-workers ring and see their forges glowing; or you can stroll through a narrow street in the Cerameicus and watch a potter moulding a lump of clay on his spinning wheel or a vase-painter drawing a design. It may be a picture of Achilles killing Hector or of men dicing or of a riot of Maenads and Sileni. But there is one important point to remember. Those vases piled around you, about the artistry of which we rave today, were manufactured not for showpieces but for sale in one of the most fiercely competitive markets of the ancient world. Attic pots had to be good pots. Their beauty of form and design is incidental, though not accidental. They were made by craftsmen who took pride in their handiwork.

In addition to direct sales from producer to consumer, there were a swarm of retail traders, called *kapeloi*. They were to be found in the stalls of the Agora, or market-place, or in the shops round about. We read of confectioners, slave-dealers, fishmongers, vintners, and the like, and of pedlars who carried goods out through the countryside. To the Greek, however, a middleman was always faintly suspect as a parasite on the body public. Thus, Aristotle says of retail trade in his *Politics* that it is a 'kind of exchange which is justly censured; for it is unnatural and a mode by which men gain from one another'.

RHYTON BY THE BRYGOS PAINTER
C. 480 B.C.

Most of the retail traders were *metics*, that is, resident aliens. The craftsmen were a mixture of *metics*, slaves, and Athenian citizens. In their hands, then, was the bulk of the production and much of the retail trade in Athens. We ought to note that there was a special 'potters' market'.

Such craftsmen-cum-shopkeepers were not, so to speak, tied to a time-clock or to punching a single button on an assembly-line. They were freemen who took time off whenever they liked. Socrates, the teacher and inspiration of the philosopher Plato, was a stonemason. Yet in the Platonic dialogues we find him in the

gymnasia or in the streets or at the festivals or at dinners, continually questioning the people he met in an insatiable search for truth. There was only one Socrates. Yet it is clear that his fellow-craftsmen were, on the whole, more interested, as long as they could make a simple living, in recreation or in politics or in discussion or in a stroll with a friend, than in piling up possessions. Yet these were the men who executed the perfect and intricate workmanship of the Parthenon, the Hephaesteion or Theseum, and the Erechtheum. As Marquadt once remarked, with the Greeks every handicraft was an art.

For the building of such imperishable monuments as the Parthenon, which took nine years to complete, the State hired quarrymen, transport-workers, carpenters, masons, goldsmiths, and sculptors. Sometimes a piece of work was let out on contract. At other times the men were paid directly by the State. Sculptors got the same wage as masons. So did slaves.

The whole picture of basic Athenian industry, except for the silver mines, implies a different set of values from our own. The craftsmen knew their trade, whatever it was, though their tools were of the simplest. Yet, in general, they seem to have preferred a full participation in the life of the city to being tied too long to any manual occupation or to getting ahead financially. From the Erechtheum inscriptions of 409 B.C. we know that the usual rate of pay was a drachma a day. A drachma—which is six *obols*—was worth on a gold basis roughly twenty cents, but in terms of today's money would probably be worth about $4.00. From other references in Greek authors it can be estimated that it cost a single man about 120 drachmai a year—or $480—to live, and a married man with two children double that amount.

The major point, though, is that the Athenian workmen could, and apparently did, have plenty of leisure time. It would take a single man only a little more than two days of work a week to earn a living.

In passing, it ought to be mentioned that there were a few cases of mass-manufacturing. In Plato's *Republic* the discussions are supposed to take place in the Peiraeus at the home of Cephalus, a rich *metic*. Cephalus, we learn, manufactured shields and employed, apparently, 120 men. Moreover, the silver mines at Laureion were let out by the State to individuals who worked them by means of slaves. Nicias, the rich man and general who, more than any other single individual, was responsible for the disaster which befell the Athenians in Sicily, is said to have rented out a thousand slaves to the silver mines.

Apart from these few instances, the craftsmen of Athens

supplied most of the home market. In the case of the potters, they also furnished an important article for export. Pottery was the dinnerware of the ancient world; but it was also used for storing every kind of liquid and dry goods—and pottery was always getting broken. So there was a fierce competition between Corinth and Athens for the pottery market of the Mediterranean. In the fifth century B.C., Attic red-figured vases won the battle.

For its export trade which, in addition to pottery, consisted chiefly of the export of olive-oil, wine, figs, and armour, Athens needed bankers, wholesale traders, and merchant-skippers. Most of these were *metics*.

Sparta periodically expelled all foreigners within her boundaries. Athens, under Pericles, encouraged strangers to settle. *Metics* could not vote or hold office and had to be represented in the law-courts by an Athenian. Yet they paid taxes which included a special head-tax per family of 12 drachmai, or $48. They were selected for liturgies, about which more will be said, and served in the army and navy. Like the Athenian citizens, they seem to have been proud of the city, and they were of tremendous assistance to banking and foreign trade.

The primary function of the bankers, or tablemen as they were called, was to change coins. By Periclean days, they were also well advanced in taking in money on deposit and in making loans. Pasion, the famous fourth-century B.C. banker, began life as a slave to a banker. Then he married his master's widow and took over the bank. At his death his assets were fifty talents or, in terms of modern purchasing power, about $1,200,000. Of this amount eleven talents, or somewhat more than a fifth, were on deposit.

The minimum interest rate was twelve per cent. On loans on ships or on ships' cargoes the rate ran up to twenty or thirty per cent; this because of a provision that if a ship was lost at sea or captured by pirates the loan was cancelled. Aristotle, again, has hard words for the banker. 'The most hated sort [of money-making] and with the greatest reason,' he writes, 'is usury, which makes a gain out of money itself. . . . For money was intended to be used in exchange, but not to increase at interest.'

Without the banker the wholesale trader or *emporos* would have found it difficult to operate. The method of the *emporos* was to buy a large consignment of goods and to hire space on a ship for it to be taken from city to city in search of a market. If successful, the wholesale trader would come to own his own ship and would become a merchant-skipper or *naukleros*. No sailing was done in winter. But each spring the merchant-skippers would load their round-bellied tubs—a Greek merchantman could carry only about 7,000 bushels of wheat—with olive-oil and wine in Attic jars and with the finest of Attic vases. Shields, spears, and helmets might be part of the cargo. So might jars filled with beads, necklaces, and other trinkets—this for trade with backward people.

Then the skipper would set out for a season's adventuring from port to port. He might, for example, unload at Massalia, now Marseilles, and take on hides and cheese, trade these at Carthage for rugs and cushions, exchange these at Naucratis in Egypt for ivory, papyrus, and linen, and so on. Or he might move into the Black Sea to bring back, finally, a cargo of wheat. Meanwhile, that same spring, other ships would be setting out from Miletus, Syracuse, Cyrene, Corinth, Carthage, and the other Mediterranean ports, with the same sort of trading venture in mind. Everywhere there would be warehouses in which the merchants could display their goods. Everywhere they would have to pay customs dues—at Athens these were two per cent on all exports and imports—and harbour tolls.

It was in this somewhat hit-or-miss but adventurous fashion that the trade of the ancient world was carried on. By this method the products of all known countries flowed into the Peiraeus, the port of Athens. The combination of her trade supremacy and the tribute from her empire made Athens one of the richest of the Greek cities of her day.

It was a very modest wealth from the modern point of view. The total annual state revenue of Periclean Athens in peace-time was probably close to 1,000 talents, or about $20,000,000 in terms of its purchasing power today, and that is about the annual budget of a fair-sized Canadian city.

During the Peloponnesian War the tribute from the empire was raised and resort was had to the *eisphora,* or direct property tax. Even in peace-time, though there were no schools, hospitals, or old-age pensions to drain the public purse, the treasury had to take care of the public festivals such as the Panathenaea and the two Dionysia—which were drama festivals—and of the huge program of non-productive public works, such as the Parthenon. In addition, from 17,000 to 20,000 of the 43,000 citizens 'ate state bread'—that is, they were on public service and were paid for it.

Their pay was not large. Jurymen, for example, got two and later three *obols* a day—that is, from $1.30 to $2.00 a day. *Hoplites* received four *obols* or $2.70 a day, sailors and marines only three *obols*.

And so one might go on. Athens could scarcely have balanced her budget, had it not been for the liturgies. These were of various kinds, of which two are of particular interest. In the *choregia* a rich man was picked to collect, maintain, instruct, and equip one of the many choruses needed, for (among other forms of art) the drama. This might cost him as much as half a talent or from $10,000 to $12,000. The *trierarchia* was more expensive. In it a rich man had to pay the cost of operating a *trireme* for a year. The cost was between two-thirds of a talent to a talent.

All citizens who owned property worth more than three talents—or from $60,000 to $70,000—were subject to the liturgies. In the first years of the Peloponnesian War, the generals were able to find 400 *trierarchs* a year.

The liturgies were a capital tax on the rich, both citizens and *metics*. Yet we learn that in Periclean Athens the holders of them competed against each other to provide the best-trained chorus or the most splendidly equipped *trireme*.

The Athenians were not in love with poverty. Pericles himself in his *Funeral Speech* observed: 'We think it no disgrace to confess to poverty but a disgrace to make no effort to overcome it.'

UNIVERSITY PRINTS, BOSTON

DANCER FROM THEATRE OF DIONYSUS, ATHENS
NATIONAL MUSEUM, ATHENS
HELLENISTIC

But the whole training of an Athenian encouraged him to put simple recreations and an active life of the imagination above possessions; and he also took it for granted that citizenship involved duties as well as rights. Our next task is to consider how his system of government contributed to these attitudes.

4

THE WORLD'S FIRST DEMOCRACY

SOME FIVE HUNDRED YARDS west of the Acropolis of Athens is a small hill. That hill is called the Pnyx. Pnyx means a place where people are packed close together. The Pnyx is where the Assembly of the world's first democracy used to meet.

If today's visitor to Athens climbs that hill, he will see on its north-eastern flank a terrace hewn out of the stone and the remnants of massive walls. Close to the summit is a huge cube of rock. The cube rests on a stepped platform. If our visitor takes his stand on that platform and faces north-east, he may not know it but he is standing where Pericles, the Olympian statesman, and Demosthenes, the persuasive orator, once stood. From this platform, as from a stage, the leaders of ancient Athens used to speak to the all-powerful Assembly, which would be packed on an artificial hillside in front of them.

If we could be transported back to the fifth or fourth century B.C., this hill of the Pnyx would look quite different. To the north-east would be the Agora, or market-place. To the right, as now, the Parthenon would gleam on the Acropolis. If we swung to our left, there would be the harbour and the sea. But on the cube of rock there would be an altar to Zeus Agoraios—that is, to Zeus, the Guardian of the Assembly. On either side of it there would be tiers of seats for the Councillors of Athens. In front of the platform, where the hill now slopes downward, an embankment would rise, supported by a retaining wall.

There would be no seats on that artificial hillside. Otherwise, the effect would be of an enormous and almost semi-circular theatre; but one which was open to the sky. The whole area covered about two-and-a-half acres. It could accommodate roughly 18,000 people sitting, or 25,000 standing. The Athenian Assembly could, and did, meet elsewhere, in the Agora, for example, or at the Peiraeus. But until about 340 B.C., its customary meeting-place was the Pnyx.

The Greek name for 'assembly' was *ekklesia*, from which the word 'ecclesiastical' is derived. The Ecclesia, or Assembly, was the final repository of power in ancient Athens. But before we examine its powers and procedures we need to take a look at the rest of the governmental machinery. This comprised, fundamentally, the ten tribes, the magistrates, and the council of 500.

Let's take a glance at the first of these divisions, the ten tribes. The ten tribes were territorial divisions of Attica, like

ZEUS OR ASKLEPIOS
ALBERTINUM, DRESDEN
5TH C. B.C.

38

miniature provinces. Each tribe was split into thirds, called *trittys*. One *tritty* of each tribe was in the mountains, a second was on the shore, a third in the plain. The original reason for this curious arrangement, so we are told, was to eliminate faction fights between the men of the Hill, the Shore, and the Plain.

Each tribe was also divided roughly into ten *demes*. The *demes* were the building-blocks of the Athenian system. Each *deme* had a *demarch*, whom we might term a 'mayor', and it had, as well, a sort of 'town-hall'. The *demes* kept the registers of citizens, handled their own local affairs as our municipalities do, and conducted elections, call-ups for the army and navy, and so on. The *demes*, then, were both the electorate and the local administrative units. The Athenians used magistrates and the Council of 500 for the general administration of the whole state.

Let's look at the magistrates first. They were both the officials and the civil service of the state. For the Athenians believed that as many of its 43,000 citizens as possible ought to participate in the actual job of administering Athens and her empire. Consequently, the magistrates held office for one year only and could not fill the same office a second time. By and large they were in boards of ten—this, so that each board could have on it one member from each of the ten tribes. By and large, too, they were selected by lot. Each board of magistrates had its own definite sphere of action.

A glance at the nine *archons* will illustrate the method of selection by lot. The word *archon* means 'ruler'; and originally, once the kingship was abolished, the *archons* had been the chief magistrates.

All nine *archons* were selected by lot from 500 candidates elected by the *demes*. To pick the nine, white and black beans were mixed in a jar. The candidates in turn thrust in their hands and came out with a bean. The first nine to get white beans were *archons* for one year only.

The functions of these *archons* were chiefly judicial and religious. The real heads of fifth-century B.C. Athens were the ten generals, one from each tribe. The generals were not picked by lot. They were elected by the Assembly and could hold office time after time. It was as one of the ten generals that the brilliant Pericles dominated Athens from 461 B.C. to his death in 429 B.C. Yet he was not a dictator. To retain his power he had to be re-elected each year by the Assembly of citizens. Only once did he fall out of favour. That was in 430 B.C. when the Great Plague, coming on top of the war with Sparta, had almost shattered Athenian morale. The Athenians voted Pericles out of office and fined him; but soon afterwards they elected him general again.

Certain other officials, such as the water-commissioners and the wheat-commissioners, were also elected by popular vote. But the great bulk of the magistrates were picked by the lot system. There were boards to look after the market, the harbour, the revenues, the festivals, and so on. All in all the number of officials rose to 700 for Attica and to these must be added the many magistrates needed to administer the empire. When you consider that all these were appointed for one year only, and that they could not succeed themselves, you will realize again how many Athenians, at some time in their lives, must have served in some official capacity. You will also understand what Sir Alfred Zimmern means when he says that Athens was governed by 'a rapid succession of amateurs'. The Athenian system was very different from our practice of a permanent civil service.

Yet there were safeguards. For one thing, a man with experience on one board could be picked by the lot for another. All prospective magistrates, too, had to pass a test for physical and mental fitness. Furthermore, once each month the Assembly reviewed the actions of the magistrates; and any one of them could be immediately suspended, as Pericles was in 430 B.C. Suspension could mean prosecution. Finally, at the end of their year of office, each board of magistrates had to submit its accounts to the Assembly and present a statement of what it had done. The Athenians kept a close and suspicious eye on their magistrates.

Next, let's turn to the Council of 500. This Council of 500 exercised a sort of general supervision over the business of the State. The 500, fifty from each tribe, were picked by lot from 5,000 candidates elected by the *demes*, and a man could serve twice as councillor. Councillors had to be over thirty years of age. They, too, were subject to the Athenian tests for physical and mental fitness. Because 500 is too large a body to act efficiently, the year was divided into ten periods, called *prytanies*, and the fifty councillors of each tribe, in turn, took charge for a tenth of a year each. Of this fifty, one-third, in rotation, had to be on duty day and night. Thus, Athens always had a government sitting. From the third of the fifty, a new president of Athens was picked by lot, each day; but the same man could not be president twice. In ancient Athens, a citizen had a very good chance of becoming president at some time in his life, even if it was only for one day. The president was chairman of the Council and of the Assembly when it met.

The Council of 500 supervised the magistrates. It had certain restricted legal powers. It arranged for the elections. It managed day-by-day finance. It received foreign embassies. One of its major duties was to prepare the business for the meetings of the Assembly.

You will have realized by this time that what is called the 'direct democracy' of Athens was not altogether a simple town-meeting form of government. The Council was, in effect, a steering or resolutions committee for the Assembly; and there was a provision that no business could come before the Assembly unless it had first been discussed in the Council. Furthermore, by law, the Council had to post the agenda, or as the ancient Greeks would say, the *programma*, five days before each meeting of the Assembly.

So now, at last, we are ready to turn to the real governing body of Athens, the Assembly. To it belonged all Athenian males over the age of twenty. After 451 B.C., to be an Athenian citizen a man had to be born of Athenian parents on both sides. At the beginning of the fifth century B.C. regular meetings were held once each tenth of a year. By the close of the century, the one had risen to three or four; which meant a meeting about once every ten days or so. To vote, a citizen had to be present in person.

Suppose we take a brief glance at one of these meetings on the hill of the Pnyx and see Athenian democracy in action. The slanting rays of the just-risen sun will be lighting up the Parthenon. The air may well be a bit nippy. Already there will be a scattering of Athenians seated on the hillside in front of the speaker's platform. They will be gossiping with their neighbours and hugging their *himatia,* or wrap-arounds, about their knees. Others will be coming down the steps from the single entrance. Their citizenship will already have been checked by six officials, and woe to the non-citizen who tries to slip past. There will be farmers who have got up long before sunrise to trudge into Athens. The citizens from the Peiraeus will have walked the four miles from the harbour. Then, there will be the craftsmen and shopkeepers from the city itself, crowding down the steps in clumps to collect in groups on the hillside. Blacksmiths, farmers, potters, merchants, cobblers, rich property-owners, sausage-makers, tanners—these are all members of the Athenian *demos,* or people, assembling here to pass on matters of routine business or of high policy.

But we must remember that this gathering is not as inexperienced in government as a similar assembly in our own country might be. Many of these Athenians have held posts as councillors or magistrates; and most of them will already have discussed the items on the *programma,* or agenda.

If the agenda is routine, there may be fewer than five thousand on the hillside. If there is something important in the wind, such as whether or not to make an alliance with Corcyra or to send an expedition against Syracuse, that hillside will be packed.

The sun rises higher. The gathering gets impatient. Then, at last, the councillors file in. The Scythian slave-police take their positions. There is a sacrifice and a prayer. The herald reads the customary curse against any orator who speaks under the influence of bribery or corruption. The chairman takes charge. The first item on the agenda is read.

Business, by the way, is divided into sacred, profane, and foreign affairs. But the Assembly has the power to demand that any item must go to the top of the list. The Council cannot use the trick of putting contentious matters at the end of the agenda, so that, when people are weary, something can be slipped through.

Along with the first item on the agenda is read the statement of the Council about it. This can be either a simple statement of the facts, or two alternative proposals on the matter, or, as was more usual, a definite recommendation as to what to do. If the Council makes a recommendation, a vote is first taken by show of hands to see whether it will be accepted without debate. In this way routine affairs can be speeded through. If the Assembly votes for debate, then the herald cries: 'Who wishes to speak?'—and the argument begins. Each speaker, in turn as he reaches the platform, is crowned with a wreath to show that, in our parlance, he has the floor. The audience is a critical one. There will be boos, cheers, and a huge-throated guffaw if the speaker mispronounces a word. The speaker can support or oppose the resolution before the Assembly; or he can amend it; or he can add a rider; or he can make a counter-proposal; or he can move that the matter be referred back to the Council for further study and a new recommendation at the next meeting.

It has already been noted that there were no political parties, except that the rich and the conservative were likely to be opposed to democracy and to favour 'oligarchy', the rule of the few. Apart from this basic division of the citizens, each speaker who has either popularity such as that of Alcibiades, or the confidence of the people such as Pericles possessed, has, as we have already seen, his coterie of followers. All proposals, incidentally, have to be reduced to writing.

When all the speaking is done, the vote on the motion or on

UNIVERSITY PRINTS, BOSTON

DEMOSTHENES
VATICAN, ROME
C. 280 B.C.

the amendment or amendments to it, is taken, again by a show of hands.

And so the day goes on. At sunset the meeting breaks up, the councillors file out, the people go home. Parliament, as it were, is dissolved until the next meeting.

There is not space for more than a brief glance at the Athenian legal system. The Council, as we have seen, had certain restricted legal powers. The Assembly could, and, at times, did act as a court. In general, however, the Assembly delegated its judicial powers to 6,000 jurymen over thirty years of age, called *dicasts*. These *dicasts*, 600 from each tribe, were picked by lot. They were paid at first two and later three *obols*, or $2.00; this was about enough to look after their board and lodging. The comic poet, Aristophanes, in his *Wasps*, has an elderly juryman describe how his daughter pets him when he gets home and his wife gives him the best of everything until his three *obols* have been cozened away.

There were plenty of cases for the jurymen to handle. There were commercial suits. There were all the cases which came in from the empire. There were the disputes in Attica itself.

Suits were divided into public and private actions, a division which corresponds roughly to our criminal and civil cases. Private actions such as disputes about property or contracts first went before a board called The Forty—four from each tribe. The Forty selected an arbitrator. You might note that, by law, all Athenian citizens when they reached their sixtieth year belonged to a board of arbitrators. The arbitrator tried to bring the contending parties to an agreement. If he failed, he gave his verdict. If the verdict was refused, he sealed it in writing along with all the evidence given in two caskets, one for each side, called, for some reason, the 'hedgehogs', and returned the case to The Forty. The Forty could settle all disputes under ten drachmai, or $40. The rest had to be sent to the courts. By this sensible arrangement many cases were settled outside the courts.

Public suits were offences such as theft, assault, or treason. Here the State did not prosecute, as with us. Instead a private citizen prosecuted. The first step was to summon the alleged offender before the proper magistrate—or drag him there if he were, for example, a thief caught in the act. If the magistrate was satisfied with the prosecutor's statement he arranged for a preliminary examination. At this preliminary examination all the evidence on both sides was collected including depositions from witnesses and citations from the laws. This evidence, along with the accusation and the denial, was sealed up in 'the hedgehogs' and, once again, no new evidence could be introduced. Then, the case went to the courts.

We are at last ready to take a brief glance at the jurymen and the courts. The nine *archons* and their secretary first selected by lot which case was to go to which of the ten courts. Then they picked jurymen by lot for each of the ten courts. The jurymen were so selected that each jury had representatives from each tribe on it. All this procedure was to guard against bribery.

You may wonder why 6,000 jurymen were needed for ten courts. The answer is that Athenian juries were mass juries. Civil suits involving less than 1,000 drachmai, or about $4,000, used 201 jurymen; if over that amount the jury was 401. In criminal cases there were the same mass juries, even up to 1,001 jurymen or more for a single trial.

Other features of the Athenian court procedure would be strange to us. The presiding magistrate could not sum up. He was a chairman and nothing more. Nor were there any lawyers. In Athens both the prosecutor and the defendant had to speak in person and conduct their own cases. Each side was assigned a definite time by the water-clock; but this was stopped while depositions were read. The prosecutor and the defendant could not cross-examine witnesses but could question each other. Hearsay evidence was not admitted. When the trial was over the jury voted at once without consultation; and its verdict was final, except that a witness of the winning side could be prosecuted at a separate trial for perjury. If that suit were won, the original verdict was quashed.

In civil suits the loss of the case was, as a rule, the penalty. In public suits, conviction in some cases brought a penalty fixed by law. If there was no specified punishment, the same jury which had found the man guilty took their seats on the benches again. The prosecution asked for one punishment, the defence suggested another. The jury voted for one of the two. Thus, when in 399 B.C. Socrates the philosopher was found guilty of impiety, the prosecution asked for death. Socrates said that what he really deserved was free living in the town hall for the rest of his life, but his friends had suggested that he pay a fine of thirty *minai*, or $12,000. The jury voted for death.

There was one exception to the power of these popular courts. All cases of homicide were referred to five special courts. This was because the shedding of blood was regarded as a pollution on the State.

I hope I have been able to say enough about the Athenian legal system to indicate that it was no primitive arrangement but a highly complex and sophisticated development. Its one great fault was the mass juries. Such juries could be influenced by appeals to emotion. Defendants brought in their children and their relatives, weeping and in rags. Yet the juries did provide judgment by one's peers and they did, once again, assure that Athenian citizens took part in running the state.

How are we to estimate the world's first democracy? It is clear that it could work only in a small state. It is also evident

THE DEATH OF SOCRATES. 1787
METROPOLITAN MUSEUM OF ART, NEW YORK (WOLFE FUND, 1931)

DAVID. 1748—1825

that under poor leadership the Athenian Assembly would tend to inconsistencies in policy. Any mass gathering is liable to be influenced by demagogues.

Yet any democracy is peculiarly susceptible to the quality of its leadership. Furthermore, though a Pericles is infrequent, the sort of democracy which the Athenians used did manage to acquire an empire and to rule it with a remarkable degree of efficiency. Moreover, the Athenian democracy did hold out for twenty-seven years against Sparta. We should not cavil, by the way, at the failure to give women the vote. Woman suffrage is a late-comer in the democracies. Furthermore, the restriction of the franchise did, at least, make the ancient Athenian prize his citizenship and the vote.

The most obvious difference, perhaps, between our democracies and the Athenian, is that in Athens the citizens did the governing, not through representatives, but in person, as jurymen, councillors, magistrates, and finally as citizens, in an Assembly where each man cast a direct vote on policies, laws, and regulations. The result was a constant, instead of a sporadic, interest in politics. In such a system there was no time-lag between what the people willed and the carrying out of that will—and no handing over of hot potatoes to Royal Commissions. There was no Cabinet rule, either. If a politician made promises, he was expected to carry them out. So, for example, when Cleon criticized the failure to capture the Spartans who had been trapped on the island of Sphakteria, he was promptly given the job of capturing them— and, as it happened, he carried out the job. By the same token, the Assembly was ruthless toward leaders who failed. When Thucydides, the historian, as a general, lost the city of Amphipolis in Thrace, he was exiled.

The main point, however, is that the Athenian democracy was a true government of the people, by the people. As Pericles observed, the Athenians called a man who did not take part in politics not 'quiet' but 'useless'.

Nor were politics dominated by financial considerations. This was, in part, because Athenian economics were less complex than ours. It was also, as the Old Oligarch, the foe of democracy, points out, because of a definite attempt to keep the rich from getting too rich. In other words, the objective was an economic democracy as well as a political one. A further and a very definite ideal was freedom. Aristotle believed that democracy was a perversion of constitutional government, though the least objectionable of the perversions. Yet even he was forced to admit in his *Politics* that 'the basis of a democratic state is liberty'.

Thus, Pericles claimed that Athenians respected and observed the laws. But he also pointed out that 'we have no black looks or angry looks for our neighbour if he enjoys himself in his own way'.

Consequently there was no censorship in fifth-century B.C. Athens. Rather there was an almost unparalleled freedom of speech as well as of thought. In the midst of the bitter war against Sparta, Aristophanes was permitted to satirize the generals of Athens, and the great Pericles himself, on the stage, and to plead for peace. He was not put in jail. Instead he won first prizes. Furthermore, as Sir Richard Livingstone points out in his *The Greek Genius,* there was no attempt to make people 'good' by social legislation. Periclean democracy trusted humanity. It believed rightly or wrongly that, given the opportunity, humanity will on the whole choose the better instead of the worse.

The freedom which the Athenians enjoyed was a rare thing in antiquity—or, for that matter, in modern times. That feeling of freedom was, perhaps, the chief reason why Athenians, to paraphrase Pericles, fell in love with their city, and why Athens became an education to Hellas and the world and not a little of the tremendous outburst of art and literature in fifth-century B.C. Athens must be attributed to the liberty in speech, thought, and action which its citizens enjoyed.

The bell-like keynote of the world's first democracy was freedom.

5

THE GREEKS AS WRITERS AND ATHLETES

'GREEK, SIR,' said Dr. Johnson, 'is like lace; every man gets as much of it as he can.'

The world has changed since Dr. Johnson's day. Few people nowadays learn Greek, and to that extent the world is the poorer. Yet Greek literature, even in translation, has much to offer. It is the well-spring of Western letters. Furthermore, in its clarity of thought, perfection of form, directness and humanism, Greek literature, like the Parthenon, is an eternal achievement of the mind and the spirit.

Greek literature can be considered from many points of view; and in any appreciation of it an ounce of reading, even in translation, is worth tons of talk. In this brief sketch an attempt will be made to indicate some of its principal types in the hope that a glimpse of the essential qualities of what Sir Richard Livingstone calls 'the Greek genius' will shine through.

'All things,' the Greeks themselves used to say, 'begin with Homer.' To them, Homer was 'the blind old man of Chio's rocky isle' who composed the *Iliad* and the *Odyssey*. Both poems are woven around the war against Troy, which was captured by the bronze-armoured Achaeans about 1184 B.C.—yet, as has been noted, Homer himself is thought to have lived about the middle of the ninth century B.C. Memories of Mycenean days are, therefore, inextricably mingled with the customs and manners of Homer's own era.

In the *Iliad*, Homer relates one episode of the war against Troy. That episode is *The Wrath of Achilles*; and Achilles was the greatest of the Greek heroes. The wrath is set going when the leader of the Greeks, Agamemnon, takes from Achilles, his sweetheart, Briseis. Here is a universal motivation, one which anyone can understand; and from that incident, the Wrath spreads wider until it 'burns in a world that is on fire'. For, on the other side is the Trojan hero, Hector, a man of dogged courage and of deep affection for his wife, Andromache, and his son, Astyanax. Hector kills Patroclus, the friend of Achilles. Achilles, who had withdrawn from battle, returns to avenge his friend. From that time forward until Hector faces Achilles, the tension mounts. Meanwhile, through the mist of war, always beautiful, always self-deprecating, moves that figure who brings doom to all, Helen of Troy. The *Iliad* is primarily about people.

RED-FIGURED KYLIX (EXTERIOR): SACK OF TROY
LOUVRE, PARIS

BRYGOS PAINTER.   FIRST QUARTER OF V CENT. B.C.

It shows the glitter of battle. It also touches on the tears which lie behind the panoply of war.

The *Iliad's* world is, as one would expect, a primitive world. Ethics are simple. Gods and goddesses, motivated by the same impulses as humanity, mingle freely with men.

But there is little that is primitive about the technique. There is the metre which flows as smoothly as a running brook or thunders as majestically as Zeus himself. There is the rich broidery of the Homeric simile and the Homeric epithet. Phrases such as 'trailing-robed Trojan women' or 'seaward-swimming river' or 'crooked-gaited oxen' build pictures. The whole poem is noble in its motivation and rapid in its action. There is no shrinking from facts. Both the bad and the good in humanity are revealed; but with no lip-smacking lingering on the ugly or the diseased. Instead, there is a detached objectivity. When Achilles finally strikes down Hector and, in refusing the dying man burial, wishes he could bring himself to eat Hector's flesh raw, we feel the shock of the brutality. Yet, later, when Priam, Hector's father, comes to beg for the dead body of his son, Achilles receives him with generosity and pity. The essential qualities of Greek literature are already present in the *Iliad;* and the *Iliad* begins European and Western literature.

Homer's second epic, the *Odyssey,* is equally fascinating but in a different way. The story is about the homecoming of the crafty Odysseus from Troy.

Homer composed epics about kings and nobles for an audience of nobles and kings. But the world changed. A depression set in and Hesiod, the pedestrian writer of the didactic or teaching epic, for farmers, is the expression of it. 'Let not a flaunting woman coax . . . and deceive you; she is after your barn,' is one of his sour maxims in the *Works and Days*.

After Homer, the centuries from 800 to 500 B.C. were years of flux for the Greeks. As we have seen, they swarmed out over the Black Sea and the Mediterranean. Kings disappeared. Merchants rose up to battle for power. Tyrants seized their moment. Oligarchy and democracy stepped on stage; and a new poetry arose to mirror the changing age.

That poetry used new metres. All of it was set to music and it was often danced as well. All of it, too, was short and all of it breathed an intense immediacy. In part, this new poetry was the expression of a vivid individualism. Archilochus, for example, cast his invectives with such savagery that, according to legend, the girl who had rejected him and her father both hanged themselves. Alcaeus flung forth his songs of wine and revolution. Sappho sang of love so frankly and directly that her nine books were burned by the Byzantine churchmen. Yet the two odes and the fragments which remain are so pellucid that she is ranked as the greatest of poetesses. Of one poem, only two lines remain. Even in translation they have a poignant simplicity.

O evening star, that bringeth back all that bright dawn hath scattered;
Thou bringest the sheep, thou bringest the goat, thou bringest the child back to its mother.

In Sappho's poetry is both the bright dawn putting shining toes on the mountain-peaks, and the haunting nostalgia of headlands black against an evening sky. Side by side with this simple lyric of passionate individualism, there sparkled the choral lyric. This song-dance poetry was an expression of the newly emerging city-state. The king of choral lyric is Pindar. His odes to honour victors at the Olympic and Pythian games marry vivid imagery and flashing metre. His poetry also ushers in the Golden Age of Greece—the fifth century B.C.

To that century belong the two founders of history—Herodotus and Thucydides. Herodotus was a man from Halicarnassus in Asia Minor, who travelled the ancient world with the mind of an adult but the fresh wonder of a child. Later, he paused from his roamings in Periclean Athens. His history purported to be the story of the Persian Wars. But Herodotus

UNIVERSITY PRINTS, BOSTON

BRONZE "SAPPHO"
FROM HERCULANEUM
MUSEUM, NAPLES
LATE HELLENISTIC
C. 50 B.C. TO 50 A.D.

desired to amuse as well as to instruct and his method was to report everything as he heard it; though he does add that he did not, necessarily, believe all that was told to him.

Thus, he begins his history with a travelogue of the Persian Empire, and he crams it full of anecdotes and strange customs. There is Egypt and Babylon as Herodotus himself saw them back in the fifth century B.C. From him you can also discover that Danube islanders get drunk on smells; or that Egyptian cats jump in the fire; or how Babylonians make sure of marrying off all their maidens. For, says Herodotus, once a year the most beautiful of the marriageable girls are auctioned off to the highest bidders; and then this money is given to the men who are willing to wed the ugly ones. You can also read enthralling short stories, such as how Gyges came to be King of Lydia or how the clever thief came to marry the King of Egypt's daughter. Everything he saw and heard was ink for Herodotus' pen. Yet, withal, there is, finally, a stirring and highly personalized account of Marathon, Thermopylae, Salamis, and the rest of the great struggle between the Greeks and Persians; and Herodotus' credibility is, today, more valued than it used to be. There are few books in any language which make more fascinating reading than the history of Herodotus.

Thucydides, the Athenian, was an historian of a different cast of mind. With him, modern history is born. He wrote of the great war between Athens and Sparta, in the hope that his work would be a possession for all time. There are acute observations on human conduct. His attempts to get at the truth and at the motivations behind events are obvious. Thucydides was convinced of what Santayana was to say later: 'Those who cannot remember the past are condemned to repeat it.'

The writing of scientific history was begun by Thucydides. Western drama also owes its beginnings to the Greeks. The first European tragedy was produced in Athens in 534 B.C. by Thespis, and the word 'thespian' enshrines his name. After him came in rapid succession three Athenians who were also three of the greatest tragic poets of any time and any age. These three were Aeschylus, Sophocles, and Euripides.

Aeschylus was the thunderer, the man who had fought at Marathon. His tragic effects are cumulative—gloom piled on gloom—and his style is majestic, replete with bold metaphors and with what the comic poet Aristophanes called 'bolt-fastened words'. His preoccupation was with the problem of the suffering of the innocent. His explanation was that a rich and powerful man, in a state of satiety, commits an act of *hubris* or arrogance.

This *hubris* lets loose doom upon the man and all his family until either the family is wiped out or expiation is made. Aeschylus' one surviving trilogy, the *Oresteia,* is an exposition of this theme.

Sophocles, however, is more of an artist than a preacher. His verse is smooth, his tragic structure almost perfect. He uses what Aristotle calls the *peripeteia* or reversal of fortune. In his *Oedipus Tyrannus,* for example, the tragic hero, Oedipus, surmounts all obstacles, until at the moment of truth his own success smashes him down to destruction. What Sophocles taught was, above all, the inevitability of destiny; but in the *Oedipus Tyrannus* the tragedy is all the more poignant because, throughout, Oedipus' motives are noble.

The third tragedian, Euripides, is the sceptic, the rationalist, and the iconoclast. He brings on stage women in love. He shows gods acting in a jealous and unworthy fashion. He punctures the conventional ideas of his day. He also gave Western drama the five-act structure and the mechanical prologue.

From what has been said it can be seen that tragedy was, in a way, the pulpit of Athens, for drama was a religious festival in honour of the god Dionysus, who was also the god of the grape and of immortality. There were rural festivals in Attica at which choral dance-songs and drama were put on. But the two great occasions in Athens each year were the Lenaea or Lesser Dionysia at about the end of January and the Greater or City Dionysia around the end of March. At the latter, three tragic poets were picked to compete. Each presented three tragedies and a satyr-drama. The satyr-drama was an obscene play to commemmorate the fertility aspect of the god Dionysus. In addition, at that same festival, three—or possibly five—comic poets were selected to present one play each. When we consider that between them Aeschylus, Sophocles, and Euripides wrote over three hundred plays of which we have only thirty-three left, and when we consider all the other poets who competed and who have left behind them only a few fragments, we can realize how much of Greek literature has been lost.

DIONYSUS,
"SARDANAPALLOS"
VATICAN, ROME
C. 350-330 B.C.

But what of the theatre in which all these plays were produced? Greek theatres were on hill-sides and were in the open air. They regularly seated from 15,000 to 20,000 spectators. Yet the acoustics were excellent.

At Athens, the stone ruins of the theatre of Dionysus still rest on the south slope of the Acropolis Hill. Those ruins, however, belong to a theatre which was built around 340 B.C. and was later remodelled more than once. The fifth-century B.C. theatre was on the same site but its seats and stage were of wood. It could accommodate from 18,000 to 20,000 spectators.

Let's suppose we are in that theatre in the centre of the topmost row of seats, early on a morning of late March in 442 B.C. The sun will be peeping over the range of Hymettos. Below us, in a great three-quarter circle, descend row after row of seats. They will be filling up rapidly as citizens and foreigners pour in. In Athens the dramatic festivals are public holidays and there is a fund from which the poorer people are provided with two *obols* to buy a place. Prisoners are even released from jail to attend. There are women, too, gay in wrap-arounds of saffron, golden-brown, frog-green, and plum-purple. Their hair will be elaborately coiffured, their faces touched up with eye-shadow, face-powder, and rouge, and many will be twirling parasols against the sun. Some will be carrying lunches. At Athens plays go on continuously from sunrise to sunset.

At the bottom of the tiers of seats, and partly embraced by their wings, is a circular floor. This is the orchestra. In Greek this means dancing-floor—and that's just what it is. Here the

UNIVERSITY PRINTS, BOSTON

THEATRE OF DIONYSUS, ATHENS
GREEK. ROMAN RECONSTRUCTION.
LARGELY C. 330 B.C.   REBUILT I—III CENT. A.D.

chorus will sing and dance—but the chorus usually represents fifteen old men. In the centre of the orchestra is an altar to Dionysus to remind us that this is a religious as well as a dramatic festival. Behind the orchestra is a long, narrow stage with, probably, one or two broad, shallow steps to connect it with the orchestra. Between the stage and the projecting ends of the tiers of seats are two entrances for the chorus. The background of the stage represents, as a rule, a palace front, so that the orchestra and stage are thought of as a palace courtyard. Furthermore, there is no curtain. Thus, the Greek dramatist had to compose his plays knowing that all his action must take place in a palace courtyard with no change of scene. This meant that happenings indoors or off-stage had to be reported—and hence the importance of the messenger-role in Greek tragedy. Furthermore, the lack of a curtain meant that there was no way to indicate a change of time. The action of Greek plays had to take place within twenty-four hours. As a result there could be little or no development of character.

It is remarkable that in spite of these limitations the Greek playwrights could produce such gripping tragedies.

The other face of drama—comedy—was, in fifth-century Athens, bawdy, intensely personal in its attacks, and completely uninhibited. Yet, if you read the plays of the great comic poet, Aristophanes—and they are well worth reading—you will note that they, too, preach. Aristophanes attacks war. He assails the new education and the Athenian law-courts. In *Women in Parliament* he argues that women could govern Athens better than the men do—a revolutionary notion for his day and age. To appreciate Greek drama, one should read it.

In the fourth century B.C., literature changed. Philosophers wrote and taught and Greek New Comedy came into being. The New Comedy, via the Latin playwrights Plautus and Terence, became the ancestor of Western comedy.

After the conquests of Alexander the Great, with Greek culture spread over the whole of the Near East, the climate of letters changed again. Realism, cosmopolitanism, didacticism, antiquarianism, obscurantism, and the notion that 'a big book is a big nuisance,' were some of the new features of literature. Study-poets wrote what was called 'the little epic'. Yet the charming *Idylls* of Theocritus, in praise of scenery and of country-songs, set going pastoral poetry; while, as a compendium of all the new tendencies, there was a great interest in the epigram. To the Greeks the epigram was not a short, pithy statement with a sting in its tail, but any short poem in elegiac metre. There

were lush love-epigrams as well as poems of artistic appreciation
and of satire. And who can resist the wry humour in the epigram
which translates as follows:

> I, Dionysius of Tarsus, lie here at sixty,
> Having never married—and I would my father had not.

VISIT OF DIONYSUS TO A DRAMATIC POET
NATIONAL MUSEUM, NAPLES
HELLENISTIC PERIOD

Greek literature is at its best from Homer to Aeschylus,
Sophocles, and Euripides. There is perfection of form. There is
idealized realism, a detached objectivity, a complete frankness
without any touch of morbidity, and a directness and humanism
which enthralls—and yet the whole is infused with passion, even
if the emotion is restrained. Like good musicians, Greek writers
did not always pull out all the stops. 'Sow with the hand and
not with the whole sack,' was one of their proverbs.

Before the Greeks, athletics—which is a Greek word—were in
general performances put on by professionals as entertainment.
The Greek view, however, was that everyone should participate
in athletics, not for pay but for the honour and joy of the
competition—and, besides, they believed that a healthy body was
as important as a sound mind. Hence, athletics were a regular
part of their school curriculum; and hence, too, the popularity
of athletic festivals all over the Greek world.

Of these festivals the most important, naturally, were the
Olympic Games. These were established in 776 B.C. in honour
of Zeus, with a wreath of wild olives as the prize for a victory.
No non-Greek could compete; and each contestant had to prove

that he had had six months' training and was free from any moral stigma. Furthermore, there was a sacred truce during the games. In addition to athletics, there were competitions in horse-racing, drama, music, and poetry. The Olympic Games were held once every four years at Olympia in Elis, which is in southern Greece.

To them came contestants and spectators from all over the Greek world—so that they became, like the modern Olympics, a sort of huge fair. To the Olympic Games were added during the sixth century B.C. three other great national sports events—the Pythian, Isthmian, and Nemean games at, respectively, Delphi, Corinth, and Nemea, in honour of the gods Apollo and Poseidon and the hero Hercules. The prizes were, in order, wreaths of laurel, pine, and parsley.

These four national games were the topmost peaks of Greek athletics. But almost every Greek city-state also had its own local annual athletic festival. Like the Great Games, they were religious events, in honour of a god.

One of the most famous of these local festivals was the Panathenaea at Athens. Every fourth year the Panathenaea reached special heights. In addition to athletics, horse-races, and a regatta, there were musical contests, recitations, torch-races, war-dances, and even a beauty contest—for the best-looking male. Such festivals, by the way, included events for boys and youths as well as for men. In Sparta there were athletic contests for girls and young women as well as for men.

BRONZE ATHLETE
VICTORIOUS FROM
BENEVENTO
LOUVRE, PARIS
5TH C. B.C.

All contestants competed entirely nude. As a by-product, the Greek games gave an impetus to the sculpture of first the male and then the female nude figure.

For our knowledge about Greek sports we depend on evidence from literature, archaeology, sculpture, and vase-paintings. In the sixth century B.C. boxing and wrestling were to the fore and the strong man was the ideal. Milo of Croton, so the story goes, developed his muscles by lifting the same bull-calf every day, so that when it was full-grown he could still carry it. The father of the famous boxer, Glaucus of Carystos, is said to have discovered his son's prowess when he saw him hammer in a ploughshare with his naked fist. More solid proof of strength comes from a block of red sandstone at Olympia. The block weighs 315 pounds. On it is a sixth-century B.C. inscription which reads: 'Bybon threw me over his shoulder with one hand.'

In the fifth century B.C., however, the ideal athlete was the all-round sportsman. The supreme victor at the Olympics was now the man who won the *pentathlon*—that is, the five contests. These were running, throwing the discus, throwing the javelin, jumping, and wrestling.

In running, the primary races were the *stade* and double *stade*—that is, about 200 and 400 yards respectively. The word 'stadium' comes from the Greek measure of distance, the *stade*. In each case the runners had to start with their feet in grooves seven inches apart. No crouching start was permitted and style as well as speed was judged. There were also long-distance races of up to three miles, and races in armour. It might be noted that Greek runners were said to be able to chase down hares; while Herodotus tells us that the Athenian, Pheidippides, covered the hundred and fifty miles from Athens to Sparta in two days.

Throwing the discus and the javelin were similar to our events, except that the Greek discus could be either of stone or of metal and seems to have varied in weight from three to fifteen pounds. There was no Greek running high-jump. The usual jump was the broad- or long-jump. The Greeks used a take-off point and a dug-up landing-pit as we do. They also utilized jumping weights or *halteres*. These *halteres* weighed on an average two-and-a-half pounds. Experiments have shown that, employed properly, they increase the length of the jump. But we do not believe a Greek epigram which says that Phayllus of Croton jumped fifty-five feet or about twice the distance our best broad-jumpers can reach.

In the Great Games, wrestling was limited to what the Greeks called 'upright wrestling'. The objective was to throw your opponent to the ground.

These were the events of the *pentathlon*. Boxing was also popular. Greek boxers wore, not gloves but what were called the 'soft thongs'. These were strips of ox-hide wound round the knuckles to protect them. In the fourth century B.C. the soft thongs were replaced by the 'sharp thongs'. Here, there was a ring of hard leather around the knuckles and a sort of glove to protect the hands and wrists. A blow from one of these 'sharp thongs' would be like hitting a man with a knuckle-duster. Later on, the Romans loaded the ring around the knuckles with lead. This was called the *caestus*. A sculpture from Herculaneum shows a battered and seated boxer, armed with the *caestus*, looking up over his shoulder as he waits for the contest to begin.

The most brutal of all Greek sports was the *pankration*. Here two men fought each other in a sort of all-out wrestling in which anything went, until one of them gave in. Toe-holds,

BRONZE BOXER FROM
OLYMPIA
NATIONAL MUSEUM,
ATHENS
C. 325–300 B.C.

BOXER (BRONZE)
TERME, ROME

c. 100 B.C.

strangling, hitting and jumping on an opponent were all fair play. Only gouging and biting were forbidden, and even these, the Greek author, Philostratus, tells us, were permitted in Sparta. The ancient Greeks loved beauty—but they were also tough athletes.

You will note that the Greeks preferred track and field sports. They did practise a few team games. On the sixth-century base for a statue, which is now in the National Museum at Athens, field or ground hockey is, quite evidently, depicted. In the centre two players are facing off with a ball, while on each side are other players with field-hockey sticks. There is also a man who seems to be the referee. On the same base is a game that looks something like rugby. Two players in the centre appear to represent the line. On one side a man is getting ready to throw a forward pass with a small ball, while on the other a player has his arm extended as if to catch it, while still another appears ready to block him.

We know that this game was called the 'team game', that a white line was drawn across the centre of the playing-field, and that behind each team was a goal-line. The object of the game, a Greek author named Pollux tells us, was to throw and, probably, carry the ball until one side was forced back over its goal-line.

The fifth century B.C. was the high point of Greek athletics. In the schools boys were taught athletics. In the gymnasia young and old alike participated in sports. But in the fourth century professionalism began to take over, the object being to win the valuable prizes offered by local sports events, such as the Panathenaea. Theagenes of Thasos is said to have carried off 1,400 prizes by travelling from one sports event to another.

The ancient Greek achievement beggars words. They began our literature, and what they wrote has never been surpassed. They set our standards in such diverse fields as politics, architecture, sculpture, and athletics. As we shall see, they began Western science and Western philosophy. On whatever road modern man sets his footsteps, in almost every case, an ancient Greek has blazed the path.

6

THE TORCH OF GREEK THOUGHT

EARLY IN THE SIXTH CENTURY B.C., a Greek lit the torch of free inquiry. That Greek was Thales of Miletus in Asia Minor. Instead of accepting Greek legends about how the universe came into being, Thales tried to solve the riddle by reason. In so doing he let loose the restless mind which seeks to know and is willing to follow the argument whithersoever it leads. With him, Western science and Western philosophy set foot on their adventurous roads.

The attempt of Thales was to suggest one primary substance from which the universe is derived. For this World-Stuff he chose water.

To his pupil, Anaximander, the primary substance was an indeterminate stuff which he called 'the Boundless'. Anaximander also developed further than Thales the theory of the Identity of Opposites—that is, for example, that hot and cold are differing aspects of the same essential phenomenon. Though only fragments of what he wrote have survived, we know that in a somewhat remarkable anticipation of modern knowledge, Anaximander postulated both other worlds or galaxies and a rudimentary theory of the evolution of man from fishes. This theory he supported by the collection of fossils.

The third of the Milesian thinkers was Anaximenes. His basic substance was air.

The answers to the riddle of the universe which these Milesians offered were mere fumblings. Their importance lies in the attempt to explain the universe by reason.

In that same century, Pythagoras of Samos, a contemporary of Anaximenes, introduced a mystical and metaphysical trend into Greek thought. Even to state his philosophy is far beyond the possibilities of this book. We need to note, however, that under the influence of a Greek religion called Orphism, Pythagoras postulated a pure soul confined in an evil body. As far as the universe is concerned, he thought of its primary substance being 'the Boundless'; but held that this Boundless was then parcelled out into geometric number-forms. For example, the most sacred symbol of the Pythagoreans was an equal-sided triangle of ten dots, which works out to four dots on each side, and one in the centre. These number-forms, according to Pythagoras, were the only reality and the only object of knowledge, while the visible world we see or the ideas we apprehend, such as justice, are merely reflections of these number-forms. He also believed in the transmigration of souls.

The influence of Pythagoras on the great philosopher Plato is obvious. Furthermore, from Pythagoras onward there were two streams of thought among the early Greeks, the one emphasizing a metaphysical approach to the problem of the why and how of the universe, the other tending toward a mechanistic explanation of these questions.

In the fifth century B.C. the Greek world was aboil with thinkers. The Eleatic School made reality a perfect sphere, 'uncreate, immovable, and unknowable'. To them the visible world was all illusion. Heracleitus of Ephesus postulated that everything was always changing into something else. 'You cannot step into the same river twice,' he said.

This Heracleitean flux, as it is termed, was again an interesting anticipation of a discovery of modern science. But Heracleitus believed that all things changed out of and back into fire. The way in which things changed from one substance to another was controlled, he thought, by the *logos*. This *logos* was more than natural law. To Heracleitus, there was immanent in the *logos* an element of justice and right.

Meanwhile, in Sicily, the amazing Empedocles, who was a physician and poet as well as a philosopher, was proposing universes of four elements—Earth, Air, Fire, and Water. These elements were brought together by Love or repelled from each other by Hate. At Athens, Anaxagoras was suggesting that the origin of the universe lay in an infinity of what he called 'seeds' floating in a void. But, said Anaxagoras, Mind—the Greek word is *nous*—gave a whirl to this infinity of seeds; and the clash thus produced gave rise to the world.

Anaxagoras was called 'Brains' by the Athenians and was prosecuted for impiety in 432 B.C. He escaped to Lampsacus in Asia Minor, where after his death the citizens put up an altar to Mind and Truth in his honour. In passing, we may note that, although all these philosophies ran counter to Greek religion, there were during this ferment of new ideas only four prosecutions for impiety, and only one judicial execution—that of Socrates in 399 B.C. With our own past history in mind, we must give the ancient Greeks high marks for tolerance.

The final touch to ideas such as those of Anaxagoras was the Atomic theory put forward by Leucippus and Democritus. This interesting, though rudimentary, anticipation of modern thinking postulated an infinite number of atoms—the Greek word means an indivisible unit—falling through a void. Their clash produced one universe after another and their separation destroyed and caused death. Motion, according to Democritus, was inherent in these atoms and their actions and reactions were determined by natural law. 'Nothing,' said Democritus, 'happens at random, but everything occurs according to law and is determined by necessity.'

Though all that has been given is a mere sketch of the thinking of these early Greeks, I hope that it has become clear that the Western world owes a great deal to them. Meantime, alongside these speculative thinkers, in that same fifth century B.C., the Sophists were working and talking, particularly at Athens. These men were the founders of the new education. Though they were individualistic thinkers and never formed a school, they were, in general, sceptical of conventional religion and of speculative philosophy. Like many people since, they asked: What good is philosophy? So they turned to man and made him the centre of the universe. Politics, ethics, the nature of justice—questions such as these interested them. Out of them steps Socrates.

Socrates was a Sophist and yet not a Sophist. His method and many of his interests partook of the sophistic trend. But, unlike the Sophists, he took no pay for his teaching and was not interested in success. His whole objective was the search for truth, particularly in the field of human conduct.

Suppose we take an all too brief look at this remarkable Athenian. His dates are from about 470 to 399 B.C. He was a stonemason. He was snub-nosed and ugly. He proved himself a brave soldier. As a councillor of Athens, he opposed the Assembly in 406 B.C., when he believed it to be acting against the law. When the Thirty Tyrants ruled Athens and ordered him to arrest one of their victims, he refused, though the refusal seemed to mean death.

In these respects he was a normal, high-principled man. But he believed that the god Apollo of Delphi had given him a mission to convince his fellow-citizens that, though they thought they had knowledge, they really knew nothing because only the god had wisdom. In the pursuit of this mission he developed an acute question-and-answer method. Because he left no written works behind him but only a fervent group of disciples, it is difficult to distinguish in the dialogues of Plato, which are Socrates' own thoughts and which are Plato's. Among concepts which can safely be assigned to Socrates is the providential direction of the universe, the belief that it is better to suffer

SOCRATES AND SENECA
MUSEUM, BERLIN
AFTER STYLE OF LYSIPPOS, C. 325-330 B.C.
ROMAN COPIES

injustice than to commit it, and a typically Greek notion that virtue is knowledge and sin, ignorance. If a man really knows the 'good', thought Socrates, he will embrace it. Socrates also believed that he was accompanied by a good spirit which told him what not to do.

This stonemason put a lasting imprint on Greek philosophy. He turned its attention to ethics: school after school of thought took some phase of his teaching and developed it. His most famous disciple, Plato, went on to become the giant of Greek philosophy—and, for that matter, the colossus of Western philosophy. Plato, by the way, is a nickname meaning 'broad'. His real name was Aristocles and he was of noble parentage on both sides.

Plato's dates are from 429 to 347 B.C. The shock of his master's execution for impiety in 399 B.C. sent him travelling, and particularly to Sicily and Italy. When he returned to Athens in 387 B.C. he established his famous school, the Academy, first in the gymnasium of that name and then in his own garden. That school, which became a sort of university, lasted until it was abolished by the Emperor Justinian in 529 A.D.—or, for over 900 years.

To do more than bring to your attention one or two of Plato's thoughts is impossible; for Plato's thinking developed as he grew older, and on some points scholars are still in dispute as to the real meaning of what he wrote. Furthermore, many of his concepts are so abstruse that a sketch of them is sure to be completely inadequate. With apologies beforehand, therefore, one or two insufficient and superficial statements will be made in order to bring him to your attention, in the hope that these statements will stimulate you to read him.

Plato wrote in a charming and finished style, casting his works in the form of dialogues. In the early dialogues, in particular, Socrates is the chief personage.

Plato's *Republic* is probably his most widely read work. In this he used the device of setting up an ideal state in order to see justice 'writ large'. Plato disliked Athenian democracy and rather admired proto-totalitarian Sparta. So, this ideal state is to be ruled rigidly by guardians, often called 'the philosopher-kings'. The second class are the warriors. At the bottom of the scale are the working-classes. For the two upper classes there is to be communism of property and of the sexes. Their whole and sole loyalty is to be to the state—which is to be brought into being, by the way, by what Plato calls, 'the noble lie'. The sexes are to have equal rights and duties. Education is to be state-controlled and there is to be a strict censorship of literature. Sir Richard Livingstone has pointed out forcibly how alien Plato's whole concept of the state is to the ideals of Periclean democracy. But, from time to time, it and the *Laws,* his second-best state, have exerted considerable influence on Western political systems.

The noblest part of Plato's thought is to be found in his concept of God and in his theory of Ideas. One may, perhaps, risk one or two statements about the Ideas. The Ideas are unalterable, eternal and intangible—and yet are the only true realities. Such is the Idea of Justice. Such, too, is the Idea of a perfect triangle. No matter how accurate our instruments, none of us can ever draw a perfect triangle. Yet somewhere, Plato taught, there exists the Idea of a perfect triangle which our minds apprehend. Of all these Ideas the visible world is only a series of imperfect and transitory shadows. The Ideas can only be apprehended by the mind; but the closer man comes to apprehending them, the closer he is to nobility. For at the head of the Ideas is the Idea of the Good.

Whether God Himself is to Plato the absolute Good or not is disputed. Quite clearly, God is Mind in the Absolute; and this Mind, by a complicated process, thinks the universe into existence. The important thing, however, is that each man possesses a soul. This soul comes from God and is imprisoned in

PLATO
MUSEUM, BERLIN
POSSIBLY AFTER SILANION, C. 335-330 B.C.
ROMAN COPY

the dungeon house of the body. If it finally achieves goodness, it returns to the star which was assigned to it at birth. If it lives badly, it is imprisoned in another body. The 'good life', which to Socrates was to be lived for its own sake, in Plato becomes a necessity, though he still held with Socrates that virtue equals knowledge.

To this theory of the soul is linked Plato's belief in our knowledge at birth of the good and the beautiful because of the soul's memories of them. But we soon forget what our souls have seen. In Wordsworth's words: 'Our birth is but a sleep and a forgetting.'

The grandeur of Plato's concepts has cast its influence on all Western philosophy. His pupil, Aristotle, also put a deep imprint on the West.

Aristotle came to Athens from Stagira in Macedonia. We are told that he lisped, carried a cane, and was somewhat of a dandy. After Plato's death he became the tutor of Alexander the Great. When Alexander set out to conquer the Persian empire, Aristotle founded his own school in Athens. That school was called the Peripatetics, because Aristotle lectured while walking about.

One of Aristotle's objectives was to catalogue the whole of human knowledge. So he wrote on logic, metaphysics, natural science, politics, poetics, and so on. His method was to collect all the data possible and then to draw conclusions. Thus, for his *Politics*, he analysed 158 constitutions. Of these only one analysis, the *Constitution of Athens*, remains to us.

In the *Politics*, Aristotle rejects Plato's Ideal State. What he favoured was a small, self-governing city-state, ruled by its best citizens. He criticized the Socratic dictum that virtue is knowledge, by pointing out that, at times, humanity, even when it knows the better course, will choose the worse. He likewise rejected the Platonic theory of Ideas; though it has been pointed out that in this field he remained a Platonist in spite of himself. To Aristotle, God was the 'Unmoved Mover', who exists apart as pure mind and is continually engaged in contemplation of himself. By so doing, he attracts the universe. The happy man is defined as 'one whose activity accords with perfect virtue and'—with a touch of practicality—'who is adequately furnished with external goods . . . for a complete or perfect lifetime'.

Practical, too, is Aristotle's doctrine of virtue as the middle road between two extremes. For example, in the use of money, miserliness is one extreme and extravagance the other. The virtuous man takes the middle road.

Aristotle's influence on the medieval world was tremendous. To them he was, in Dante's words, 'the master of those who know'. Whatever he laid down was accepted as second only to the word of God. Thus, by a curious paradox, the works of a man whose desire was to investigate and to know became chains to fetter free thought.

With Aristotle, who died in 322 B.C., the great age of Greek thought ends. For the conquests of Alexander the Great spread the Greeks as a ruling caste over the Near East. Out of the fusion of Greek civilization with the ancient civilizations of Syria, Egypt, and Babylonia rose a new culture which is called not Hellenic but Hellenistic. Meanwhile, three great Hellenistic kingdoms emerged—Egypt, Syria, and Macedonia. All three were ultimately gulped down by Rome.

This Hellenistic age from about 300 B.C. onwards was in some respects similar to modern times. In economics, credit capitalism developed; while in Egypt under the Macedonian Ptolemies, there was state socialism. For example, there was a state bank with branches in every town and village—and cheques were used. Furthermore, the state dictated to the peasants how

NATIONAL MUSEUM, NAPLES

ARISTOTLE. BRONZES FROM HERCULANEUM
LATE III CENTURY B.C., ROMAN COPY; AND
C. 335—325 B.C., ROMAN COPY

much land to put into each type of crop; and the peasants had
to sell their crops to the state and the state only, at a price fixed
by the state. The state, too, was the only exporter for many
articles, such as papyrus.

The Hellenistic world went in for the colossal. The city of
Alexandria, which Alexander the Great had founded in 332 B.C.,
swelled to almost a million inhabitants—a far cry, indeed, from
the tiny Greek city-states. Alexandria's library had in it a copy
of every known book. Its two main streets were a hundred feet
wide and, as an ancient author informs us, glittered with lights
'like the sun in small change'. The beams from its four-hundred-
feet-high lighthouse, the Pharos, were seen, we are told, twenty-
seven miles out at sea. To give one more example, a ship named
the *Syracusa* and built to run between Syracuse and Alexandria
was of close to 4,000 tons burden. It was furnished with luxury
cabins, fountains, and gardens; and the water in its hold could
be pumped out by one man with the force-pump which
Archimedes had invented.

The Hellenistic era is also the age of Greek science. Modern medicine had already been begun in the fourth century

B.C. by Hippocrates of Cos. Today's medical men still take the Hippocratic oath. Hippocrates, by the way, died in 357 B.C. at the age of 104. His work was advanced by dissection which led to studies of the optic nerve and the eye, to an understanding of the functions of the brain, and so on.

The great name in physics was Archimedes who discovered specific gravity and founded the science of hydrostatics. He also laid down the principles of the lever and of the centre of gravity. Among his inventions were cogged wheels, the compound pulley, and pneumatic machines. His machines, in fact, destroyed a Roman fleet which was besieging Syracuse. When the Romans, after three years, captured Syracuse, a soldier accidentally killed Archimedes.

HIPPOCRATES (MALE PORTRAIT STATUE)
MUSEUM, COS

ABOUT 150—100 B.C.

In mathematics, Euclid developed the geometry which we still use. Archimedes himself used indeterminate equations, calculated square roots, and anticipated integral calculus; while his proof of the relation of the volume of a sphere to a circumscribing right cylinder was enshrined by a design of it on his tomb. Similarly, Apollonius of Perga did a monumental work on conics, and in the second century B.C. Hipparchus developed trigonometry.

The achievements of the Hellenistic Greeks in astronomy were even more startling. As early as the fourth century B.C. Heracleides of Pontus had found out that the earth revolves on its axis once every twenty-four hours—and you will note that at this time there was no medieval nonsense about the earth being flat. In the third century B.C. Aristarchus of Samos advanced the heliocentric theory—that is, that the earth and the planets revolve around the sun. The Greeks held a conference about it but, unfortunately, the geocentric theory won out. Yet the discovery of the name of Aristarchus on the margin of a Copernican manuscript suggests that Aristarchus gave the clue to Copernicus and Galileo.

A contemporary of Aristarchus, Hipparchus, a man who has already been mentioned, measured with precision the length of the year, the size of the moon's disc, and its distance from the earth. A first-century B.C. Greek, Posidonius, tried to do the same for the sun, but arrived at only ⅜ and ⅞ of the correct figures. Yet these were tremendous achievements for men who lacked even a telescope.

Meanwhile, Eratosthenes of Cyrene, who lived from 273 to 192 B.C., had measured the earth's circumference and was only 195 miles out. This same man discovered that Europe, Asia, and Africa are really one big island and stated that if you sailed west far enough you would reach India. It was this statement which filtered down to Columbus and started him off in 1492 A.D. Columbus, as you know, was headed for India and, as it were, ran into North America by mistake. Yet a Hellenistic Greek had already suggested that there might be a continent to the west of Gibraltar.

Among minor inventions of these Greeks are listed slot-machines, catapults and water-organs operated by compressed air, a fire-engine, and a toy steam-engine. In both pure and applied science the Greeks made a long stride forward in the Hellenistic period—and it was this period which influenced Rome.

In philosophy, however, which was now more or less separated from science, it was a search for a way of life rather than an objective inquiry into the why and how of the universe. For in the Hellenistic world the individual felt naked, alone, and futile. 'We are all watched and fed for death like a herd of swine butchered wantonly,' wrote Palladas.

In consequence, the Hellenistic era was the age of clubs and societies of all kinds, of mystery religions promising personal salvation and immortality, and of the philosophic brotherhoods. Of these philosophic brotherhoods, three had a definite impact on the Romans. These three were the Stoics, the Cynics, and the Epicureans.

Epicurus founded his philosophy in his garden at Athens about 306 B.C. To give a very summary account of his teaching, he believed that pleasure was the road to happiness; but his highest pleasures were the pleasures of the mind and his happiest man was the serene man who avoided excess.

Epicureanism made a number of Roman converts. Horace, the famous poet, called himself 'a fat porker from Epicurus' herd'. A generation before him, Lucretius, in a noble and evangelical poem, the *De Rerum Natura,* expounded the doctrines of Epicurus. Along with a vicious onslaught on religion, he included an elaborate description of evolution.

The second of the two philosophic brotherhoods was Cynicism, begun by Antisthenes, a pupil of Socrates. In brief, his view was that the most virtuous man was he who had the fewest wants. 'I would rather die than feel pleasure,' said Antisthenes. Cynicism was originally so named because it was taught at Athens in the gymnasium called the Cynosarges.

The most famous of the early Cynics was that Diogenes who went around Athens at noon with a lantern in his hand, looking for an honest man. Later the Cynics, in practice, are scarcely to be distinguished from the Stoics. Like them, they preached the fatherhood of God and the brotherhood of man. In the first century of our era they put on a missionary drive to become 'the mendicant monks of paganism'.

The appeal of the Cynics was to the unlettered crowds. Stoicism was the favourite philosophy of the upper-class Romans.

Stoicism was begun by Zeno from Citium in Cyprus. About 300 B.C. he taught in Athens in the Stoa Poikile, which means the Painted Colonnade. Hence came the name Stoicism.

The Stoics were essentially moralists. Virtue was the chief end of life—and virtue was to be attained primarily by indifference to pleasure and pain and, indeed, to all the emotions. They therefore chose a cosmogony which would back up their belief. In this theory there was a Fire-Soul which permeated all the universe. Thus man himself had a spark of the Fire-Soul enclosed in the fleshly envelope of the body. 'God is within us,' was a favourite Stoic saying.

The aspiration of the individual soul was to rejoin the World Fire-Soul; that is, Stoicism, like Hinduism, craved not personal immortality but release from the 'Wheel of Life'. Their code of ethics was based on the belief that the soul of him who yielded least to human emotions remained the most pure. So they were ascetics. To them the truly 'wise man' would be equally happy whether he rotted in a dungeon in chains, or sat 'on the golden throne of Nero'.

When one looks back over this very incomplete and superficial account of Greek thought, one realizes how much the Greeks have contributed in philosophy, science, and ethics, both to the Romans and to ourselves. The greatest value of the Romans to us, perhaps, is that they preserved for us so much of Greek culture. Greek ideals of art and beauty, Greek ideas, and Greek freedom of thought—all these lie at the very foundations of Western civilization.

UNIVERSITY PRINTS, BOSTON

GREEK WAR DANCE
VATICAN, ROME

FIRST CENTURY B.C.

7

THE ROMAN WORLD

ITALY IS A SEVEN-hundred-mile-long boot, eternally poised to kick Sicily out of the Mediterranean. Its 91,000 square miles is close to four times the size of the Greek peninsula and it is far richer. About half its area is in the huge and fertile valley of the Po River. Though the Apennines dominate the rest of Italy, their slopes and valleys were, in ancient times, thick with forests. On the western coast, too, are the plains of Tuscany, Latium, and Campania. Wheat, barley, timber, orchards, the vine and the olive, herds of cattle, sheep, goats, and swine—all these, in terms of ancient economy, made the country rich. Its scenery offers the almost impossible blues and greens of the coast-line from Cumae and Naples southward, the bare and rugged colours of the hill-top towns and the turquoise of its Alpine lakes. Its climate varies from north to south—and from lowland to upland.

Such, in brief outline, is the land in which Rome was to come to power. Rome itself owed its beginnings to a river, a ford, and the Seven Hills. For, in very early times, there was a vigorous trade in salt from the mouth of the Tiber along the river to the tribes of the interior. Some sixteen miles from the Tiber's mouth, navigation ends. At this same point an island makes a ford possible and low hills give shelter. This is where Rome began. The Romans put the founding of their city in a year which by modern dating is 753 B.C. But excavations have proved that the first primitive settlements on the site of Rome go back to before 1,000 B.C.

Those first settlers may have comprehended that the Seven Hills controlled both the river traffic and the north-south trade by way of the ford. For that matter, in Roman times the road from Rome to the Sabine Hills was still called the Via Salaria, which means 'the salt-road'.

But these first inhabitants of Rome could not have foreseen that the site of Rome made it natural for her to become the mistress first of Latium and then of Italy. For Rome on the Tiber is about half-way between the sea and the hills, and the plain of Latium—which is roughly forty miles wide and twice as long—is close to the centre of Italy.

In 753 B.C. Rome was a small community. Its people, the Romans, were Latins mixed with Sabines. The Latins spoke an Indo-European language, which they called the *lingua Latina*, the Latin tongue. Down the centre of Italy, through the Umbrian, Sabine, and Samnite country, were other Indo-European tribes.

All these peoples were blond intruders from the north, and were cousins to the Greeks. In Venetia and in Iapygia, on the east coast, were Illyrian settlers. In Liguria, which is in the north-west of Italy, and on the fringes elsewhere, were dark-skinned Mediterranean stocks.

Indo-Europeans, Mediterraneans, Illyrians—all three were in a primitive stage of culture. For civilization, as you know, began in the Near East, and the harbours and plains of Italy are on the west coast. Civilization came to Italy later than it did to Greece. When it did appear, it was brought by Carthaginians, Greeks, and Etruscans.

The Carthaginian influence was never very strong. But the Greeks made a lasting, and in the end, the major imprint. Starting as early as the eighth century B.C. they planted their colonies in Sicily and fringed Italy with settlements from Brindisi around the heel and toe of the country to as far northward as Naples and Cumae. In Sicily the Carthaginians checked them. In Italy the Etruscans blocked their expansion to the north.

The Etruscans are a mystery people. The usually accepted view is that in the eighth century B.C. they landed on the west coast, north of Rome, in that part of Italy which is still called Tuscany after them. They were highly civilized. It is thought that they came from the east. As the decades went by, they reached out northward over Umbria and into the valley of the Po. Mantua is one of their foundations. So is Milan. Later they were to be pushed out of the Po valley by an onrushing surge of the yellow-haired and Celtic Gauls.

Before that time, however, the Etruscans had also moved south over Latium. Rome was for a while an Etruscan city. When, in 509 B.C., it became a free republic, there was little hint of the splendour that was to come. Rome had lost the hold on Latium which the Etruscans had given her. Her total territory was about ten miles by twenty-five.

For roughly a century, Rome fought a savage struggle for mere survival. Fortunately, she soon became once more the leader of the Latin League of Latium. But there were the savage hill-tribes to the east and south. To the north were the Etruscans. Then, just after Rome had captured the Etruscan city of Veii, the Gauls raided south. Before the fierce rush of these blond giants who fought naked except for shields and swords and gold torques around their necks, the Romans broke. Rome was

WRESTLERS (FRESCO)
TOMB OF THE AUGURS, TARQUINIA

ETRUSCAN PAINTING. VI CENT. B.C.

sacked and burned.

But the Gauls withdrew and, luckily for Rome, they had weakened the Etruscan power. Stubbornly, the Romans started again. In desperate war after war they finally, by 272 B.C., became the unchallenged masters of all Italy south of the Po Valley. But, no sooner was this achieved than Rome was pitchforked into two climactic conflicts. These were with Carthage. When in 202 B.C. Hannibal was beaten at the battle of Zama, Rome emerged as the despot of the western Mediterranean. Spain, Sicily, Sardinia, and Corsica were her possessions, and she had moved northward to the Alps. The Roman empire had begun.

During this same period, until 287 B.C., there had been vicious internal strife in Rome between plebeians and patricians. The plebeians achieved political, economic, and social equality. Yet one result of the Carthaginian wars was to place a new nobility of wealth and office-holding in control of the Roman state. Thus began what is called the Rule of the Senate—which was a permanent body of some three hundred magistrates and ex-magistrates. Meanwhile, there was still a distinction between the Romans, the original inhabitants of Rome, the Latins of the plain of Latium, and the Italians. This distinction was later on to disappear.

It was in those three centuries of constant warfare that the character of the early Roman was formed. A people struggling for survival have little interest in philosophic speculation or in the search for beauty. Harsh, unbending discipline, dogged endurance, narrow bigotry, devotion to the practical—these were the qualities which were needed. The ideal Roman virtues were simplicity, seriousness, dignity, and piety—by which last they meant the proper performance of one's duty to the gods, to the state, and to one's family.

Such people can only understand what they can grasp and hold. Yet, when they came into contact with Greek culture they recognized its superiority. It was in 272 B.C. that the Romans captured the Greek city of Tarentum, which is now Taranto, on the instep of Italy. The Greek prisoners became the tutors of the Roman children. And thus was begun the process by which, to quote the famous cliché, 'captive Greece took her rude conquerors captive'. That trend was intensified by Rome's conquest of Greece and the Hellenistic Near East.

After the desperate struggle against Hannibal, which dates from 218 to 202 B.C., the Roman people deserved a breathing-space. Instead, they were plunged into wars with Macedonia, and with Antiochus the Great of Syria. There was a third Carthaginian War which ended in the obliteration of Carthage. Spain revolted, but the rebellion was crushed. By 133 B.C. the Romans were the unchallenged masters of the Mediterranean. The empire was now established.

On the whole the conquest of the Near East was merely a training exercise for the Roman legions which were, by this time, the most efficient fighting-machine the ancient world ever devised. The Romans discovered that war could be made to pay. It was in 168 B.C. that Aemilius Paullus crushed Perseus, King of Macedonia, at the battle of Pydna in northern Greece. The celebration of the triumph of Paullus in Rome occupied three days; and no less than 250 wagons were needed to carry the plunder—art, arms, silver, and four hundred crowns of gold from the Greek cities. After Pydna, the war-tax was not levied again in Italy until 43 B.C., the year after the assassination of Julius Caesar. Between 200 and 150 B.C. over a hundred tons of silver poured into Rome.

So, the loot of the Near East flooded into Italy—gold, silver, paintings, statues, jewel-studded tables, golden thrones, and the like. Above all, there was a host of war-captured slaves.

In that flood of wealth the old Roman character began to dissolve. Banking and capitalism sprouted and flourished. The ruling class, the senators, were either sleeping partners of the capitalists or, like the Verres whom Cicero prosecuted, used the governorships of the Roman provinces to plunder those provinces. Self-indulgence became the rule.

In 62 B.C. Julius Caesar owed twenty-five million *sesterces*.

UNIVERSITY PRINTS, BOSTON

CICERO

VATICAN, ROME

SECOND CENTURY A.D.

JULIUS CAESAR: BUST IN MARBLE

MUSEUM, BERLIN; MUSEUM, NAPLES

ABOUT 50 B.C.; ABOUT 98—117 A.D.

A *sesterce* is usually estimated conservatively as worth five cents in today's money. On that basis Caesar owed $1,250,000. Later, he is said to have bought a single pearl at $300,000 for Servilia, the mother of that Marcus Brutus who, in 44 B.C., helped to assassinate him. Similarly, Cicero, who was only moderately well-to-do, could own six villas and buy a house for $175,000. Cicero also paid $25,000 for a single table of citrus-wood. The villa of Scaurus at Baiae, the pleasure-spot north of Naples, was valued at a million-and-a-half dollars. The gardens and banquets of Lucullus became a proverb. The Romans still paid lip-service to the old Roman virtues. In practice, they who in the early days had taken even their pleasures sadly became gross and greedy materialists.

But the enormous wealth was limited to a small class. The main mass of the Romans and Italians were either starving peasants or debt-ridden farmers or people on the dole. Italy had become, as the historian Mommsen puts it, 'a society of beggars and millionaires'. Meanwhile, Rome's republican constitution, which had been framed to govern a small city-state, creaked and groaned as it strove to administer an empire.

POMPEY
GLYPTOTHEK, N.Y.,
CARLSBERG, COPENHAGEN
1ST C. B.C.

PHOTO. ARCHIVIO VATICANI

AUGUSTUS, FROM
PRIMAPORTA
VATICAN, ROME
C. 20 B.C.

The result was a century of internal struggle. When Julius Caesar defeated Pompey the Great, it seemed as if ravaged Italy might have a rest. But Caesar's assassination in 44 B.C. set off a new round of civil wars. When in 31 B.C. Octavianus, the adopted son of Julius Caesar, defeated Mark Antony and Cleopatra at the battle of Actium, the Romans gladly gave up political freedom for a dictatorship which assured tranquillity. Octavianus, as Caesar Augustus, became, in effect, the first emperor of Rome.

And then for two centuries, from the battle of Actium until the death of Marcus Aurelius in 180 A.D., the Roman empire experienced a peace and prosperity such as the world has seldom seen since. True, there were frontier wars. In the last century of the republic Pompey had tightened Rome's hold on the Near East and Julius Caesar had conquered Gaul. The battle of Actium added Egypt. During the first century A.D. there was rectification of the northern frontier and Britain was conquered. The Emperor Trajan occupied Mesopotamia and what is now Roumania; Mesopotamia was soon relinquished, but Dacia, as Roumania was called, was held until Aurelian withdrew from it in 270 A.D.

There was, too, more than one savage revolt of the Jews. In Rome itself, in the first century A.D., several emperors met violent deaths. But all of these happenings scarcely affected the security of the empire as a whole; and from 96 to 161 A.D. there was an era of almost uninterrupted peace. The ancient world lay cradled in the *Pax Romana*.

Let us take a look at that empire. From north to south, it stretched from the Great Wall in Britain, and from the Rhine, the Danube, and the Black Sea, to the Atlas Mountains, the Sahara Desert, and into the Sudan. On the west it was bounded by the Atlantic, on the east by the Arabian Desert and Mesopotamia. What is now France, Switzerland, Austria, and parts of Germany belonged to it. So did Spain, North Africa, Macedonia, Greece, and the Near East. The empire was about 2,000 miles from north to south and 3,000 from east to west. Its area was roughly two-and-a-half million square miles and its peak population is estimated at a hundred million. Thus, it was a sizeable empire for any age.

That empire was protected by the Roman fleet and the Roman army. The maximum force in the army was around 400,000 men. Under Domitian, legionaries received 1,200 *sesterces* a year or $60, plus a grain allowance. In the meantime the term of service had been increased from twenty to twenty-five years. It might be pointed out here that until Marius, just before the first century B.C., the Roman army had been a citizen army. Marius and Julius Caesar between them made it into a long-service professional army of volunteers. At discharge a veteran received a bonus of 12,000 *sesterces* (about $600).

Though the army was paid so poorly, it was the iron ring of the legions which kept the Roman world secure. Inside the empire there were great cities and prosperous municipalities with a large measure of local self-government. There were many Roman citizens. By the Social War of 90-88 B.C. the Romans had been forced to give the franchise to the Italians. By the end of the century all free men south of the Alps were Roman citizens. Julius Caesar granted citizenship to whole towns and tribes outside of Italy and to those who had served in the army, whatever their nationality, and he also planted colonies of citizens all over the empire. He even admitted provincials to the Roman Senate. Augustus was more conservative but there was an increase of 900,000 on the citizen roll during his reign. In this way Roman citizenship was widely extended. Thus, St. Paul, though a Jew, was proud of his Roman citizenship. Under later emperors, such as Trajan and Hadrian, the citizen franchise included the upper class of every city in the empire except in Egypt. Finally, in 212 A.D., every free man in the empire was made a citizen.

YOUNG MARCUS
AURELIUS
CAPITOLINE MUSEUM,
ROME
2ND C. B.C.

Citizenship helped the romanization of the empire, particularly in the west. So did the network of roads and the trade which flowed along them. The total mileage of those roads is estimated at 47,000. The oldest of them was the Appian Way, built from Rome to Capua in 312 B.C. As the Roman power reached out, so did the roads. Along them the legions marched. And along them flowed the never-ending traffic, travellers on foot, carriages, wagons transporting goods, post-horses, and the like.

UNIVERSITY PRINTS, BOSTON

BRUTUS II
MUSEUM, NAPLES
FIRST CENTURY A.D.

The Roman roads were the arteries of the empire. They were built to endure. Today, for example, you can still walk on patches of the Appian Way where St. Paul once trod.

Those roads were all marked at intervals with the distance from the golden milestone which stood in the Roman Forum. Quite literally, all roads led to Rome. Under the empire a passenger, freight, and express system was organized. For the imperial couriers, there were post-stations for the changing of horses. For the transport of goods, there were *mansiones*, which in English means waiting-places. These *mansiones* maintained riders, drivers, conductors, doctors, blacksmiths, wheelwrights, and

HADRIAN
VATICAN, ROME
2ND C. A.D.

about forty beasts and the appropriate amount of rolling stock. In this way the trade of the empire could be kept moving.

There was even a well-organized passenger service. By the fourth century A.D., first- and second-class tickets were being sold and from the first century A.D. the Romans had sleeping carriages in service. Free passes were issued, good for from one to five years or during the life-time of an emperor. Under the empire every Roman of any pretension at all was likely to make the 'grand tour' to Athens, Ephesus, Antioch, and down the Nile.

To the great roads must be added the seaways. To the Romans the Mediterranean was *Mare Nostrum*, which means 'our sea'. It was furrowed by countless round-bellied merchantmen, carrying passengers and freight.

The empire was, in fact, a paradise for businessmen. In foreign traffic, traders found their way to Denmark or up the old amber route from the Danube to the Baltic and across it to Sweden. Furs and slaves poured through the Brenner Pass into Italy. In the Near East Greek merchantmen worked their way to Somaliland and beyond and Roman traders pushed by land into Abyssinia.

The most exotic trade was to Arabia Felix, India, and China. Part of this was by caravan route from Syria, either to Arabia for spices and gold-dust or to India for gems and cottons or to China for silk. The Romans called the Chinese the 'silk people' and in 97 A.D. a Chinese envoy travelled to Antioch in Syria to establish relations with the Graeco-Roman merchants. Over a century before this, however, the first tiger to be seen in Europe since the extinct sabre-tooth variety had been brought to Samos to Augustus Caesar.

The more popular route to India and the far East, however, was from Alexandria via the Red Sea and the Indian Ocean. Each year as many as 120 ships set out for India. They carried gold and silver plate, metals, tools, weapons, trinkets, luxury goods, and Roman currency. Hoards of Roman coins belonging to the first half of the first century A.D. have been dug up in southern India. After the reign of Nero, these hoards are also found in north India. Another interesting item is the discovery of a statue of the Hindu goddess of prosperity, Laksmi, at Pompeii, the town which Vesuvius buried in 79 A.D. It is known, too, that at least one Greek merchant crossed the Malay Peninsula and sailed up the coast; while in the reign of Marcus Aurelius a group of Graeco-Roman traders reached the court of China.

From India, the Romans brought back pearls, rubies, cotton-

BRONZE EQUESTRIAN STATUE OF MARCUS AURELIUS
PIAZZA DEL CAMPIDOGLIO, ROME

161—180 A.D.

cloth, tortoise-shell, spices, teak, ebony, pepper, and Chinese silks. As we shall see later, there was no luxury the ancient world had to offer which the Romans denied themselves. But the volume of trade inside the empire was much more enormous. Where now there are a score of frontiers, there were then no barriers to free trade, no customs posts, no import dues to pay. From the Great Wall in Britain to the Sudan and to Mesopotamia there was one huge trading unit. From Britain came lead, iron, oysters, and hunting-dogs. Gaul had its own industry centring at Lugdunum, which is now Lyons. The best glass came from Egypt or from Sidon in Phoenicia. But Gaul produced glass and pottery on a large scale. From Spain, the ships and highways brought base metals, gold, silver, dyes, linen-yarns, and olive-oil. North Africa sent out slaves, gold-dust, African marble, ebony, ivory, and wild animals for the shows. Asia Minor and Syria provided woollens, purple-dyed fabrics, carpets, tapestries, leather goods, soft silken stuffs, and Damascene steel. From the Nile the merchantmen bore to Italy linens, paper, cosmetics, glass, fine jewellery, and a third of the wheat supply. Italy herself manufactured bricks, the famous Arretine pottery, and the best of steel at Puteoli, now Pozzuoli, just north of Naples—and Puteoli was the port at which St. Paul landed. The finest of wines were produced in Gaul, Italy, Greece, and Asia Minor. Apart from export and import trade, in each province there was a humming small-shop industry; while agriculture tended more and more to large estates and scientific farming. Only in Italy itself does farming seem to have declined.

From this brief sketch, I hope you will have gathered a little of the immense volume of trade and the great prosperity which obtained in the Roman empire in the first two centuries of our era. The luxury was equal to anything the world has seen since. But there was also a solid and prosperous middle-class. Banking and credit capitalism were well advanced. Cheques were used, letters of credit were common, and Roman currency was valid anywhere. When in 154 A.D. the rhetorician, Aelius Aristides, declared 'the whole inhabited world is one city-state', he was expressing the way in which the Romans had managed to weld their whole empire into one unit.

But the colossus had feet of clay. The loss of freedom under a dictatorship brought inevitable spiritual and political repercussions. The growth of a top-heavy bureaucracy and of a benevolent paternalism went unnoticed. Most of the inhabitants of the empire did not care. The extension of Roman citizenship, the levelling influence of a world-wide trade and prosperity, and the excellent government of the provinces under the imperial administration, left them contented so long as they could make money. There was slavery, but slavery was an accepted fact. There was an idle and unemployed proletariat which had to be kept quiet by doses of 'bread and games'. But the empire was an Eden for the banker, the capitalist, and the ordinary business-man. Consequently, only a comparative few cried warnings of the dangers to come. The first two centuries of our era were, in fact, as materialistic an age as any until the present. Everywhere a man was judged not by what he was but by what he owned. As the businessman, Trimalchio, said in one of the two Latin novels left to us: 'If you have a penny, that's what you're worth.'

For a brief glimpse of what life was like in the small towns of Italy during the first century A.D. fortune has left us Pompeii and Herculaneum. As you will remember, both towns were destroyed by the great eruption of Vesuvius in August, 79 A.D. Herculaneum was covered by a sea of mud which hardened to tufa rock. Consequently, it is difficult to excavate. But Pompeii was buried under a blanket of porous pumice-stone and volcanic ash; and some thirteen acres of it have been uncovered.

Pompeii was a small town with only 20,000 inhabitants. Yet when we walk its long-dead streets today, we sense a comfort and even a luxuriousness of living which modern Italian towns of the present do not possess. There were fountains in the streets. The houses were roomy and comfortable. Three public baths, with facilities which included hot-air heating, have been uncovered. There was a wide rectangular forum, paved with marble, with markets opening off it. There were two theatres and an amphitheatre. This last would seat 20,000 spectators. At one end of the forum is a temple to Jupiter; at the other, the law-courts. In one house, a set of silverplate was found, of 115 pieces. Look at it in the Naples Museum and you will note the delicacy of its manufacture and chasing. In another house a set of surgical instruments was discovered and each instrument has been identified as similar to modern ones. In still another was a statue, the Dancing Faun, and that is a masterpiece for any age. The House of the Vettii has wall-paintings by unknown artists, some of which are a beauty and a delight. Most of the houses possess delightful gardens in which fountains played; and some of them still work today. There are shops with advertising, and notices for theatre shows and for municipal elections. There are fullers' establishments and dining-rooms and tavern after tavern.

It is when we realize comfort such as this in a small town that we comprehend how prosperous Roman life was. But to understand fully the Roman standards of living, we need to compare Pompeii with Rome, the Eternal City.

8

THE ROMANS AT WORK AND AT PLAY

POMPEII AND HERCULANEUM are museums to prove the high standard of living in third-rate towns during the first century of the Roman empire. At Pompeii three municipal baths, two theatres, a basilica for the law-courts, a temple of Jupiter, and an amphitheatre are luxurious public buildings for any town of 20,000 people in any age. The shops, the taverns, the bakeries, and the houses reinforce the picture of a solid comfort and prosperity. The House of Pansa is 319 feet by 124, that of the Dancing Faun is 262 feet by 115, and these are big houses for any town or city.

All Pompeian houses face inward. When you walk into the House of Pansa today you come first into the *atrium*. This is a tall room with an opening to the sky in the centre of the roof. Beneath the opening is a rectangular pool to catch the rain-water. At the sides are rooms opening off the *atrium*. At the back is a room called the *tablinum*. This was a step above the *atrium* and could be closed off from it by curtains.

This *atrium* complex of rooms was, originally, the house in which the early republican Romans had eaten, slept, and washed dishes. By the last century of the republic, the *atrium* had become the reception hall, while the rooms off it had been transformed into expensively-equipped salons. If the family was noble, as in the case of Pansa, statues of the ancestors stood along the walls of the *atrium,* and in a cabinet in one of the wings of it were their waxen death-masks.

Behind the *atrium* and *tablinum* was a formal garden with a colonnade around it. Thus, if today's visitor to Pompeii walks through the *atrium* of the House of the Vettii—the Vettii were two rich bachelor-merchants—he will find himself in a delightful garden which is once more planted with shrubs and flowers, while all around him the fountains of 79 A.D. spout water, just as they used to do. Opening off the colonnade are the rooms in which the family lived. Let the visitor enter the room of the *amorini,* and there he will see Psyches floating on the wall; while, just above the dado, in a continuous frieze, are winged and tiny Cupids—Cupids weaving or buying garlands of flowers, Cupids at the wine-press, Cupids as goldsmiths and metalsmiths, Cupids racing in little chariots drawn by goats, and the like.

The Pompeian houses were sumptuously furnished. The floors were of tesselated marble. The wall-paintings were vivid. There were fountains, statues, tapestries, stand-lamps and candelabra, rich tables of bronze or wood or mosaic. In the new excavations there is one house with an outdoor dining-room. The Romans reclined at dinner on three couches, so arranged around a serving-stand as to leave one end open for the slaves to come and go. In this particular outdoor dining-room, a series of pierced pipes flung a cooling spray of water over the guests as they ate. In the dining-room of the House of the Moralist there is a *vomitorium* at the near end of the left-hand couch: for, as Seneca commented once about the Romans, 'they vomit so that they may eat and eat so that they may vomit'. On the walls of this dining-room are written, too, pieces of advice for the guests. One of them translates as follows:

'Do not cast wanton glances or ogling eyes at another man's wife; be modest in your language.'

It is easy to re-create ancient Pompeii in one's imagination as the home of a prosperous, gay, and materialistic people, working and playing with no suspicion that Vesuvius, which had been a dead volcano for centuries on end, would suddenly erupt. Yet Pompeii was only a small, sleepy, and backward town as compared to the teeming, hurrying cities which, from Londinium in Britain and Lugdunum in Gaul to Antioch in the east, dotted the smiling and peaceful face of the empire. Great amphitheatres still stand at Verona in Italy and at Nîmes in France as well as in scores of other places. In Switzerland and Austria are to be found the remains of Roman towns, camps, and theatres. Here and there, as at Segovia in Spain or at the Pont du Gard in France, one realizes the mighty arches of Roman aqueducts. In Crete, today, villagers still drink from fountains the Romans built. As engineers and architects, no people surpassed the Romans until the Americans of the twentieth century.

MUSEUM OF FINE ARTS, BOSTON

BUST OF ZEUS
SILVER PLAQUE
FROM LYCIA
2ND C. A.D.

But what about life at the centre, in Rome itself?

Long before the Caesars, Rome was a huge city. Under the empire it housed over a million souls. At its peak, under the Antonines in the second century A.D., the population was probably about a million and a half. It was a city of great parks, of monumental public buildings, of great palaces, and of tall apartment blocks.

Let's look briefly at the Forum, the heart of Rome. Today, there are only somewhat melancholy fragments of its former grandeur, such as the Arch of Titus, the serene ruins of the House of the Vestal Virgins, the restored Senate-House, the remains of the Rostra, the foundations of the great basilica built by Julius Caesar, and a few pillars here and there, pointing toward the Roman sky. To see it as it was in the days of the empire, we must visualize that Forum as paved and as glittering with marble, bronze, and gold. We must imagine proud statues, columns, and stately arches. We must re-create the litters and sedan-chairs of high-born women carried aloft by Nubian slaves, the conscious tread of senators and magistrates, and the milling about of a mob of people from every known land—blond Germans, wide-eyed Britons, stocky Spaniards, dark Egyptians, burly Thracians, liquid-eyed Syrians, and the rest. In front of us, if we are looking north-west, will be the temples on the twin peaks of the Capitoline. Behind us and to our left, on the Palatine Hill, will rise the palaces of the emperors.

Beyond the Forum to the east and north were the *fora* constructed by the emperors. Of these the most striking remnant is the column of Trajan. That column was erected from the spoils of the conquest of Dacia, which is now Roumania. Including the base, it is 127½ feet high. That height was to commemorate to what extent the spur of the Quirinal Hill had been levelled by the engineers. To the right and left of that column rose a Greek library and a Roman library. There was also a huge

UNIVERSITY PRINTS, BOSTON   PHOTO, ALINARI

THE FORUM ROMANUM, ROME, LOOKING EAST FROM THE CAPITOLINE HILL

LEFT: ARCH OF SEPTIMUS SEVERUS, CURIA, SACRA VIA, TEMPLE OF ANTONIUS AND FAUSTINA, WITH BASILICA OF CONSTANTINE AND S. FRANCESCO ROMANA BEFORE THE COLOSSEUM TO THE REAR.
RIGHT: COLUMNS OF TEMPLE OF SATURN, BASILICA JULIA, TEMPLE OF CASTOR AND POLLUX, HOUSE OF THE VESTALS, WITH ARCH OF TITUS TO THE REAR AND PALATINE HILL TO THE RIGHT.
ROMAN. PLAN REGULARIZED BY JULIUS CAESAR. BUILDINGS CHIEFLY I CENT. B.C.—III CENT. A.D.

basilica reached by three steps of yellow marble. Its entire floor was paved with marble and its roof glittered with tiles of gilded bronze; while today's traveller can still stare at the remains of the five storeys which, on the eastern flank, housed the 150 shops of Trajan's market.

Such is a brief hint of the magnificence of the Roman *fora*. There were other marvels for the second-century A.D. visitor to see. To the north, across the Tiber, the mighty Mausoleum of the Emperor Hadrian still stands. In the Middle Ages, as the Castel San Angelo, it served more than once as a refuge and fortress for the Popes. Further south, but north of what used to be the Campus Martius, which means 'the field of Mars', today's traveller can dine at one of Rome's more luxurious restaurants and look out at the tremendous mass of the Mausoleum of Augustus and his family. In ancient days it was a huge mound of earth on a foundation of white marble. That mound was planted with evergreens. On top was a bronze statue of Augustus Caesar.

Still further south, the ancient Campus Martius is now a mass of dwellings and shops, an area which is skirted by the main street of modern Rome. In those days it was a maze of promenades, marble porticoes, and theatres. One of Rome's circuses was there. So was its first permanent stone theatre, the Theatre of Pompey, which was built in 55 B.C. Today, the Pantheon still bears witness to the skill of Roman architects and engineers.

ARCH OF TITUS, ROME
81 A.D.

PANTHEON, ROME
ROMAN.   C. 120—125 A.D.

INTERIOR.   PANTHEON, ROME
ROMAN.   C. 120—125 A.D.   ATTIC STORY (POZZI) 1747, REPLACING PILASTERS

The Pantheon, now a Christian church, was first built in 27 B.C. by the prime minister of Augustus, Marcus Agrippa, as a temple to all the gods, but was rebuilt by Hadrian. It is a massive dome of concrete, 142 feet in height and 142 feet in diameter, with not a single pillar in between.

One could go on. There were miles of parks and gardens along both banks of the Tiber and on hills, such as the Pincian Hill, where the Borghese Gardens are the successor to the Gardens of Sallust. There was the Colosseum, which seated at least 45,000 spectators, and the Circus Maximus, which according to the Regionaries of the fourth century A.D. had 385,000 places. Even if one allows for exaggeration, it must have seated at least 200,000 people. Carcopino puts the figure at 260,000. There were also the great public baths.

Today's traveller stares in wonder at the colossal arches of the ruined Baths of Caracalla. (He ruled from 211 to 217 A.D.) If he could see them in their original splendour, he would marvel the more. Those baths at that time covered twenty-seven acres. The vast domes were resplendent with mosaics. The walls were lined with precious and coloured marbles from Egypt and Numidia. Many of the pipes, taps, and fittings were of silver and bronze. The floors were of marble. In the halls and porticoes stood famous sculptures, such as the Farnese Bull and the Farnese Hercules.

Yet the Baths of Caracalla, huge as they are, were surpassed in size by the Baths of Diocletian (emperor from 285 to 305 A.D.). His baths extended over an area of thirty-two acres. Rome's present-day Piazza dell'Esedra, where the great fountain of Neptune and the Nereids plays, was once a small part of the Baths of Diocletian. Its cold-water pool is now the vestibule of the Church of Santa Maria degli Angeli and the transept of that same church is the arch of its central hall. In another segment of those baths is housed the National Museum. The Baths of Diocletian could accommodate 3,000 bathers at one time, those of Caracalla 1,600.

Furthermore, these baths were only two of over a dozen almost as big; while, all in all, the number of baths in Rome which the public could use reached to well-nigh a thousand. Their primary purpose was for the daily bath, which was part of every respectable Roman's life. The usual procedure was to reach the baths at from two to three o'clock in the afternoon, take exercise at bowling or some form of ball, then bathe.

In bathing, a Roman undressed in the *apodyterium*, where his clothes were put in a locker. Next, as a rule, he entered the warm bath, called the *tepidarium*. After this, he took a sweat bath, and finished off by a plunge in the *frigidarium*, or cold pool. Heating was provided by hot air flues in the walls and under the floors. Up until the time of Hadrian, women often bathed and swam nude with the men.

The baths were much more than baths. In addition to the exercise grounds, they contained promenades, gardens, libraries, restaurants, concert and lecture rooms, massage-rooms, and even rooms for medical men. Their outer walls were flanked by porticoes which were full of shops. The really large baths were civic centres; the smaller ones, community halls.

Even a brief sketch of the Imperial City would not be complete without a reference to the aqueducts which supplied the baths and the palaces and the ground floors of some of the apartments. By the end of the first century there were nine great aqueducts, bringing water to Rome. The Claudian Aqueduct, whose ruined arches still march over the Roman plain, included a tunnel three miles long and three feet wide by seven in height. The arches of the aqueducts, it must be remembered, were only to carry the water-channel over plains, valleys, and rivers. Thus, near Nîmes, the Roman Pont du Gard over the River Gard is 900 feet long and 160 feet high. One can walk through its water channel, but most of the aqueduct is underground.

In these aqueducts the Roman engineers achieved a drop of as little as one in 3,000. They made traps to catch the sediment, filters to stop debris, and arrangements so that the water could be emptied while repairs were being made. When the water reached Rome, it was stored in reservoirs and distributed all over the city by underground pipes. Estimates of the amount used

UNIVERSITY PRINTS, BOSTON

ANTONINE THERMAE (BATHS OF
CARACALLA), ROME 206-235 A.D.

AQUEDUCT (ROMAN)
SEGOVIA, SPAIN
1ST C. A.D.

vary from 53 to 300 gallons per head per day for the population of over a million. Frontinus, a contemporary of Trajan, tells us that before the Trajan aqueduct was opened, eight aqueducts brought each day 222,237,000 gallons of water to Rome.

Now that the obvious monuments of Imperial Rome have been mentioned it is time to turn to the residences of the city. Rome was, like some of the great cities of North America, a mass of palaces, apartment blocks, and tall tenements.

The palaces were scattered through the city, chiefly on the hills, except that the Capitoline Hill was reserved for the two great temples of Jupiter Capitolinus and Juno of the Mint, and the Records Office; while the Palatine Hill was occupied by the emperors. The palaces were as luxurious and as spacious as the tenements were crowded and poverty-stricken. Some of the apartment-blocks, as we know from the excavations at Ostia, the port of Rome, were as roomy and comfortable as their modern counterparts. Such blocks were built round a central garden as at present. But the hollows and valleys of Rome were crowded with tall tenements in which people were hived like bees or ants. The ground floor was often given over to shops or taverns, as is again illustrated by the remains of Ostia. Above, two rooms or one, as in our modern slums, housed a whole family; while up under the tiles were lodged the poorest—so high up, says the satirist Juvenal, that if a fire breaks out down below they will not know about it until they are being burnt alive. These apartments and tenements were constructed basically of concrete; but heavy beams were used to support the flooring of the five or six storeys, and wood and brick were used for projecting balconies. Wood, rubble, and stone were utilized to make attractive facings. The stairs were of stone or wood. Windows and balconies were decked with pots of flowers.

As to the height of these blocks which were called *insulae*, which means 'islands', we know that the Emperor Augustus passed a law limiting them to seventy feet, which suggests that some were higher, and we know that that law was broken. Fires were, apparently, continually breaking out and though there was a combined police and fire-fighting force of 7,000, the fire-fighting equipment was not adequate. The great fire of 64 A.D. in the reign of Nero devastated ten of the fourteen regions of Rome and, of those ten, three were almost completely destroyed. Since the tenements were often jerry-built, and since by law the walls could not be more than eighteen inches in thickness, the buildings sometimes collapsed under their own weight. Roman builders, so excellent in their public structures, paid little attention to permanence in lower-class housing.

Among those apartment and tenement blocks twisted about sixty miles of alleys and streets. Modern Rome has many of the same type. In ancient Rome, with living-space at a premium, there were many lanes which were only six feet in width. Ordinary streets were less than fifteen feet across, though there were a few thoroughfares of from fifteen to twenty feet in breadth. Few of the lanes or streets were paved. Juvenal tells of the pedestrian who returned to his abode, mud-caked to his knees.

Even worse than the mud were the smells. The Romans had a first-class sewerage system, and at Ostia, as was true of Rome, there were elaborate public lavatories. But the sewerage system did not reach, except in a few cases, beyond the ground floor. So, from the upper floors, slops were emptied into the street.

UNIVERSITY PRINTS, BOSTON   PHOTO, ALINARI

APARTMENT BLOCKS (INSULA). VIA DELLA FONTANA, OSTIA
ROMAN. C. 150 A.D.

An even greater evil was the constant noise and the continuous mobs pouring through the narrow thoroughfares. This was chiefly foot-traffic as in modern Venice. For Julius Caesar had forbidden wheeled traffic in Rome by day except for the carts of the building contractors.

When night fell, foot-traffic ceased. The streets were unlit and robbers and gangsters lurked in the darkness. No sensible man, we are told, again by Juvenal, went out to dinner at night without making his will; and this exaggeration might be true of the poorer sections. But with night came, too, the rumbling of wagons and carts and the curses of drivers as they brought in all the supplies the great city needed—vegetables, bricks, fish, meat on the hoof, marble, timbers, milk, and similar necessities. It is small wonder that the epigrammatist, Martial, longed for his simple home at Bilbilis in Spain and finally retired to it.

And what of the people of Imperial Rome? Until the end of the republic it was relatively easy to classify them. Citizens were, in the main, of Roman or Italian stock. They were divided into senators, knights, and the plebs. The senators, the ruling class, alone had the right to wear a tunic with a broad purple stripe, an iron ring, and a pair of red sandals. The second order, the knights, were the businessmen of Rome and Italy. They wore a tunic with a narrow purple stripe and a gold ring. The common people, the plebs, had no distinguishing mark, except that only a Roman citizen could wear the *toga*. The *toga* was a voluminous wrap-around of white wool.

Those who did not have full citizen rights were either foreigners or slaves. There were numerous foreigners, naturally. Slaves had no rights.

The number of slaves in the last century of the republic and in the first century of the empire almost passes belief. It is estimated that in Rome alone, under the empire, there were 400,000 slaves.

The out-of-works had no slaves. But an ordinary man could not make do with less than eight slaves. The upper middle-class and the rich kept hundreds. They were first divided into country and city slaves. City slaves were further classified into indoor and outdoor slaves and then divided into groups of ten, such as the sweepers, the litter-bearers, the cooks, and so on. Pliny the Younger, a gentleman of moderate tastes, owned at least 500 slaves. A contemporary of his, the freedman Caelius Isidorus, when he died, left behind him 4,116 slaves. The emperors had households of at least 20,000 slaves.

The multitude of slaves corrupted the Romans. It did something more. Because of the practice of freeing slaves either during the master's lifetime or after his death—Pliny's will, for example, freed 100 slaves—the freedman class became a very important element in the population of Rome and Italy. Originally, a freedman and his sons were only second-class Roman citizens; but the grandsons had complete political rights. Under the empire, however, short-cuts became common so that a slave when freed could become at once a full-fledged Roman citizen and could reach the status of a knight. Under the Emperor Claudius, freedmen such as Pallas even joined in ruling the empire. Furthermore, Roman citizenship was conferred widely on non-Romans, and provincials sat in the Roman senate.

Thus, when we look at the Roman in the city of Rome in the first and second centuries A.D., he is more often than not no longer of Roman or even of Italian stock. After the Emperor Nerva, who ruled from 96 to 98 A.D., the emperors themselves began to come from outside Italy. Both Trajan and Hadrian, though of Roman descent, were born in Spain, and Hadrian's successor, Antoninus Pius, came from southern France.

To sum it up, then: the Rome of the empire was a completely cosmopolitan city. Apart from hosts of slaves of every nationality inside and outside the empire, the old Roman-Italic stock was swamped by swarms of freed slaves and their descendants, who had now become citizens, and by hordes of provincials —Greeks, Syrians, Jews, Egyptians, North Africans, Spaniards, Gauls, Britons—who had flooded into Rome. Many of these, too, had been granted Roman citizenship. Juvenal, the satirist, a native-born Italian, inveighs bitterly against the 'hungry Greeklings' and at the 'mud-laden torrent' which Syrian Orontes had discharged into the Roman Tiber. Even the purple-striped tunic of a senator or of a knight conveyed no assurance that its wearer was of Roman descent, and by the third century A.D. the emperors themselves were non-Romans. The Roman empire ended by almost obliterating the stock which founded it. Tenney Frank, in fact, suggests that at least eighty per cent of the population of Imperial Rome were the descendants of slaves; and by the end of the second century A.D. fewer slaves were forthcoming, since the main source of the slave supply—namely successful wars—had dried up.

During the empire, and the last century of the republic, too, there was a considerable change in the status of women. The Roman matron had always been more respected than the Athenian married woman. Matrons such as Cornelia, the mother of the Gracchi, who were chaste and only married once, were the Roman ideal. In the early republic the line between the duties of the sexes was clearly drawn. The early Roman republican worked in the fields, governed the state, and fought its wars. His wife managed the household as an equal partner in the family. But she had no standing in law. She could not bring suit in the law-courts or hold office or own property. Legally she was 'property, not a person' and her marriage was arranged by her parents. By marriage she passed from the 'power' of her father into the power of her husband. Moreover, divorce was easy for the man but impossible for the woman.

But the wealth which poured into Rome in the second century B.C. led in the next century to a class of women who were emancipated. By various legal devices they got around the prohibition against women owning property and they were as well educated as the men. Women such as Clodia, the mistress of the poet Catullus, Sempronia, the wife of Decimus Brutus, Servilia, Caesar's mistress, and Fulvia who was married to Clodius, Curio, and Mark Antony, in sequence, all held salons and influenced politics.

Under the empire this emancipation of women increased apace. Women not only owned property, they could now divorce their husbands. Juvenal states that some had had eight husbands in five years, and in his sixth satire he writes a scathing indictment against the women of his day, who do penance imposed by a priest of Isis, or fight in the Arena, or conceive passions for dancers, musicians, or gladiators. Juvenal, Suetonius, and Martial, in their lurid pictures, suggest a complete moral breakdown.

The picture they present was not true of the whole of Roman society but of only a section of the high society of the time. If we were to judge Roman society on the basis of these excesses, it would be as if we took the headlines of Hollywood excesses as a valid portrait of the whole of North American morals. For we know from the letters of Pliny the Younger and from Tacitus, the historian, as well as from inscriptions, that devoted wives and loyal husbands were rather the rule than the exception.

The world of the Roman empire in the first two centuries is almost frighteningly similar to modern North America in its excesses and its wealth and, above all, in its devotion to materialistic success at the expense of the spiritual and the intellectual. Yet it retained a hard core of solid, down-to-earth virtues and a prosperous middle-class. It was when that middle-class was squeezed out of existence by high taxes, paternalistic legislation and an ever-increasing bureaucratic control that the abyss between wealth and poverty was, at last, nakedly evident.

UNIVERSITY PRINTS, BOSTON

"PORTIA AND CATO"
TOMBSTONE OF HUSBAND AND WIFE
VATICAN, ROME
1ST CENTURY A.D.

9
Roman Luxury and Poverty

BEFORE WE CONSIDER the poverty of Rome's proletariat, and the luxury of its millionaires, we ought, perhaps, to glance briefly at the government of the empire. Theoretically, power was shared between the Roman senate and the emperor. In practice, the emperor, backed by the army, spoke the final word. From Augustus to Nerva, the cabinet posts, if we may so term them, were held by freedmen of Greek or Graeco-Oriental extraction; so that, ironically, the Greeks, who had been conquered by Rome, now administered the Roman empire. But from Trajan onward the chief positions were held by Roman knights; though these men, of course, could by this time be the descendants of slaves.

It was this sort of administration that gave to Italy and the provinces a government in which peace was maintained and in which, on the whole, an even-handed justice was meted out. Nor must we forget that the Romans encouraged a vigorous local self-government in the cities, towns and municipalities. The wall inscriptions at Pompeii testify to a keen interest in the local elections. Thus, one inscription records that 'the barbers want Trebius as *aedile*', while another tells us that his 'little sweetheart is working for Claudius as *duumvir*'.

In these local governments there was an elected board of magistrates and a local *curia* or senate, composed of the richest men of the community. Freedmen could not sit in this senate or stand for the magistracies. But they could be elected to the board of *Augustales* to carry on the worship of those emperors who had been deified. This usually happened as soon as an emperor died. Thus, on his death-bed, the Emperor Vespasian is reported to have said, somewhat wryly: 'Woe is me: I think I am turning into a god.'

This active municipal life lasted until the time of Hadrian, and so keen was the competition for office that magistrates had to pay a fee when they entered upon their term—which would be as if we made our mayors and aldermen pay for the honour of serving our cities. Magistrates, senators, and *Augustales*, and all wealthy men were supposed to make gifts to their communities. The greatest benefactors were emperors, such as Hadrian, who scattered largess across the empire. But private individuals did

their share. At Pompeii, the family of the Holconii bore most of
the expense for reconstructing the big theatre which held 5,000
spectators; and a widow, Eumachia, built an elaborate cloth-
market, just off the Forum. Similarly, Pliny the Younger, though
he was regarded as only moderately well-to-do, presented his
birthplace, Comum, now Como, in North Italy, with a library, a
school endowment, a foundation for needy children and a temple
of Ceres; while Herodes Atticus, the tutor of the Emperor Marcus
Aurelius, among other donations elsewhere, gave Delphi a race-
course, Corinth a theatre, and Athens the Odeon, or concert-hall,
which is still standing on the south-west flank of the Acropolis.

Gifts of this sort are indicative of the great prosperity of the
empire. This affluence reached to all classes except for slaves
and those on the dole. In agriculture, the trend was to large
estates. Pliny the Elder, who was killed by the eruption of
Vesuvius in 79 A.D., states that all the farming land in North
Africa was owned by only six men. Sometimes, these huge farms
were worked by slaves. Quite often they were leased to tenants,
called *coloni*.

In trade, industry, and labour, the inscriptions prove a large
number of occupations; and each occupation was organized into
a *collegium*—which may be translated as 'guild'. Thus, in Rome
there were over a hundred guilds and the inscriptions prove
similar associations in 475 towns throughout the empire. A
casual glance at the list presents us with guilds of carpenters,
horn-blowers, bakers, ragmen, gladiators, pallbearers, physicians,
porters, and even household slaves.

There would scarcely be a free worker anywhere in the
empire who did not belong to a guild. Guild members sometimes
refused to allow non-guild workers to participate in a job and
you may remember how the guild of the silversmiths in Ephesus
started a riot against St. Paul.

The guilds were in the main religious and social organ-
izations. They charged dues. An association of the humble, such
as the one at Lanuvium near Rome, asked $5.00 and an
amphora of wine as the initiation fee, while its dues were only
six cents a month. Fines were assessed, such as: 'If anyone shall
have gone to fetch wine and shall have made away with it'—
presumably by drinking it—'he shall pay double the amount.'

These guilds picked rich patrons, to present them with a
meeting-hall. As is often the case with similar associations today,
their officers had high-sounding titles, such as prefect, praetor, or
tribune. There were 'mothers' and 'daughters' of the association

and the members often called each other 'brother so and so'. Once a year, in Rome, each guild was entitled to a parade through the streets with horns, pipes, cymbals, and banners, as 'the most honourable and distinguished association' of the flask-makers or plumbers or grocers or what have you. This was followed by an elaborate picnic. Many of these guilds paid for the burial expenses of their members. They were associations for mutual help and comfort, rather than trade unions.

The inscriptions of the guilds are a welcome insight into the

UNIVERSITY PRINTS, BOSTON

CUPIDS AS WINE-DEALERS (FRESCO)
HOUSE OF THE VETTII, POMPEII

'humble annals of the poor'. For the life of the rich freedmen there is no better source than the *Dinner of Trimalchio*. The *Dinner of Trimalchio* is an excerpt from the *Satyricon*, a novel by Petronius, who was the Emperor Nero's 'arbiter of fashion'. Trimalchio is a self-made man and proud of the fact. Born a slave, he now owns estates in Italy, Sicily, and Africa, and is so rich he doesn't know how much money he has. He has bees from Hymettus in his hives and he has sent to India for mush-room spawn. He arrives at the dinner which he is giving wearing a scarlet mantle and preceded by four liveried runners. Alexandrian boys sing as they wash the feet of the guests. In fact, there's a blare of music throughout the whole dinner. There is course after course, including a boar roasted whole; but when a hunter pierces its flanks with a knife, birds fly out into the room. When the wine is served Trimalchio tells his guests: 'I had more distinguished company than you yesterday, but I didn't give them such good wine as this.'

During the meal Trimalchio is a pretentious ignoramus. He has a Greek and Latin library but gets his mythology all mixed up. He has his own poems recited. But, he confesses, what he really likes is rope-dancers and loud horn-blowing.

His friends are of the same stripe. Their one god is money. They admire a man who, in their language, is 'ready to pick a farthing from the dung-heap with his teeth'. Their talk is of the high price of bread and how much better it was in the days when Safinius was magistrate. 'You remember him,' one says, 'a red-hot pepper, not a man. Wherever he walked, he scorched the earth [yet he called] everybody by name, just like one of us.'

But a ragmaker interrupts. Cheer up, he tells his companions. 'We're going to have a first-class show, a three-day fiesta. Our Titus'—he's referring to a magistrate—'is going to give us cold steel —no running away, but butchery in full view of the amphitheatre. He can well afford it, too. His father died and left him thirty millions . . .'

It is quite clear that Trimalchio and his friends are drawn from life. The letters of Pliny do remind us that there were many urbane and humane Roman gentlemen. Yet, it is abundantly evident that the first century of the empire, in particular, was grossly materialistic.

According to Tacitus, the Roman historian, Roman luxury reached its peak in the years from 31 B.C. to 68 A.D.—that is from the battle of Actium until the death of Nero. A tremendous amount of money, it is true, was spent on Greek statues and paintings, just as American millionaires in the modern world buy up the art treasures of Europe.

Other expenditures were less praiseworthy. Trimalchio did not know how many slaves he had. This was the case with many Roman millionaires. Seneca tells of a rich man who made one slave learn all Homer by heart, another the whole of Hesiod, and others the nine lyric poets. Then, at dinner, these slaves stood behind him at dinner and gave him an apt quotation when he needed one. Each of these slaves cost $5,000. In passing, it might be noted that many slaves of rich men, such as the doorkeepers, became rich themselves from bribes.

To a people as gross as the Romans over-eating and over-drinking were as natural as breathing. The famous gourmand, Apicius, a contemporary of the Emperor Tiberius, spent four million dollars on food and drink and committed suicide because he had only half a million dollars left. Pliny tells of a man who served dishes of speaking and singing birds at a cost of $5,000 a course. One of Nero's friends poured out $200,000 on roses for one banquet alone. A single feast of Lucius Verus, the colleague of Marcus Aurelius, cost $300,000—but we must remember that at this banquet Verus gave to each of his friends gifts which included gold and silver dishes, beautiful slaves, and carriages with teams of mules and their drivers. The Roman millionaires even dissolved pearls in vinegar and drank them.

Along with luxury of the table went extravagance in furnishings. Babylonian carpets, Corinthian bronzes, costly tables, gold dishes, and crystal goblets were common, while to even the lower middle-class, silverplate was an ordinary possession. A slave of the Emperor Claudius owned one silver dish which weighed five hundred pounds.

Meanwhile, Roman matrons spent fortunes on Oriental silks, Tyrian purples, expensive perfumes, and jewels from the East. Lollia Paulia, one of the wives of the Emperor Caligula, once wore two million dollars worth of gems at a banquet—and that figure is conservative.

In an age when a freedman of the Emperor Claudius sneered that a man worth only three million dollars was 'pitiably poor', the rich indulged themselves in palaces and villas of a splendour which even our billionaires have done no more than equal. The poet, Valerius Maximus, observes that a palace covering four acres is 'cramped'. Pliny the Younger's villa at Tusculum included parks, ponds, fountains, temples, and libraries. Versailles was anticipated a thousand times in ancient Italy. There were floors of costly mosaics. Coloured and expensive marbles were shipped in from Africa and Egypt.

The summit of this form of extravagance was reached by Nero's Golden House. The modern visitor to Rome can still see a few fragments of it. In Nero's day it boasted a triple colonnade a mile long. In its vestibule was a statue of Nero, 120 feet high. There was a pond in it, on the site of which the majestic Colosseum now stands. There were vineyards, pastures, and woods, filled with wild and domestic beasts. There were rooms of which the walls were plated with gold or made entirely of pearls. The main dining hall was circular and revolved on its axis day

UNIVERSITY PRINTS, BOSTON

ROUND TEMPLE NEAR THE TIBER. ROME
ROMAN. EARLY AUGUSTAN c. 30 B.C.

and night. Yet we ought to note that even the villa of the good
Emperor Hadrian, near modern Tivoli, had a circumference of
seven miles. No people since the ancient Egyptians and until the
modern North Americans ever worshipped sheer size and decora-
tion so religiously as the Romans.

Nero also boasted 1,000 carriages drawn by horses shod with
silver and harnessed with gold. Even Nero could not equal the
extravagance of Caligula. In one year, according to Suetonius,
the biographer of the Caesars, Caligula spent 135 million dollars.
Then, to replenish his treasury, he resorted to executions, con-
fiscations, and auction-sales. One of Suetonius' more charming
anecdotes is of an auction held at what is now Lyons in France
in the winter of 39-40 A.D. At that auction a gentleman fell
asleep but nodded as he snored. Caligula told the auctioneer to
count every nod as a bid. When the gentleman awoke he had
bought thirteen gladiators for the enormous price of $450,000.

Caligula was the emperor who built a bridge from his palace
on the Palatine to the Capitoline so that he could commune with
'his brother', the god, Jupiter. Among other excesses, he had huge
pleasure-boats built, decked with baths, colonnades, banquet-halls,

PROCESSION FROM THE ARA PACIS. ROME 13-9 B.C.

and sterns studded with gems. Two of these were dredged up at Lake Nemi in the Alban Hills but were unfortunately destroyed during the last war. His favourite horse, Incitatus, was given a stall of marble, a manger of ivory, and a jewelled collar. It was said that Caligula intended to make this horse consul of Rome.

Such is a brief sketch of the gross and ostentatious luxury of Roman emperors and millionaires. At the opposite end of the scale were the beggars, the clients, and those on the dole.

In spite of a prosperous middle-class and in spite of the free labourers in guilds, the number of the poor was legion all over the empire. But poverty was most apparent in Italy and, in particular, in Imperial Rome where slaves had ousted free labour. In 45 B.C. Julius Caesar found in Rome no less than 320,000 Roman citizens receiving free grain. From Augustus onward they numbered around 200,000—and it must be remembered that these 200,000 were adult males, so that women and children must be added to the total.

These were the people who lived in the garrets and attics of Rome, a family to a single room, or slept out of doors. Along with part-time workers or hungry poets such as Martial, they crowded the halls of the rich each morning to receive the *sportula*, or dole. They were called clients. The *sportula* was at first doled out in food and Martial tells of clients who brought along portable stoves to cook what they received. But the *sportula* was given in money, too. By Trajan's time, the usual rate was thirty-one cents per client. So each morning you must imagine the halls of each of the rich men of Rome crowded with clients come to pay their respects to the great man. In return for the dole the clients were supposed to accompany their patron through the routine of the day, to the law-courts, for example, or to a meeting of the senate. But, in addition to the dole, the rich man was supposed on occasion to donate to each client a new toga and, at the Saturnalia, which corresponded to our Christmas holidays, to present him with five or six pounds of silverware.

Yet, in spite of the client system, the presence of a huge mass of unemployed citizens in Rome was a constant menace. It was met in part by the distribution each month of free grain from the great warehouses along the Tiber below the Aventine; and, naturally, the public treasury had to pay the cost of transporting the grain from Africa and Egypt and of distributing it. Each emperor, in addition, contributed money payments. Thus Marcus Aurelius dispensed altogether $212.25 to each male citizen. There is nothing new about the idea of a 'dividend' from a government to its citizens.

Feeding the unemployed was not enough. They also had to be amused. This was done by free admission to the games. The games, or *ludi*, were originally religious celebrations. By the time of Augustus, sixty-four days in each year were occupied by the games. By the reign of Marcus Aurelius, their number had increased to 135 days in the year. These were the regular festivals. There were also extraordinary games. In 80 A.D., for example, Titus presented games for 100 days in succession and Trajan celebrated the conquest of Dacia by 123 days of continuous festivities.

There were three kinds of games—the theatrical, amphi-theatrical, and the circus games. Of these the theatre shows were the least popular. The Romans were not Athenians. They did not crave thought-provoking dramas but preferred erotic or sensuous or brutal spectacles. The pantomimists, accompanied by huge orchestras, danced Leda and the Swan, or Orestes pursued by the Furies; and the mime replaced comedy. The mime, in which women did the strip-tease, was on a par with American burlesque, except that, on occasion, tortures and killings were enacted to the life on the stage.

The shows in the great Circus Maximus, however, never lost their appeal. If today's visitor to Rome stands on the south-western rim of the Palatine Hill, facing the Aventine Hill, he will see beneath him an oval valley. To get the picture of the Rome of the Caesars, he must imagine running down the centre of that oval an immense *spina*, or backbone, of marble. On it will be shrines and statues and an obelisk from Egypt. That obelisk now stands in Rome's Piazza del Popolo. At both ends of that *spina* will be the gilded goal-posts and behind these at one end seven bronze dolphins and at the other seven eggs in cups on top of seven pillars. Around the *spina* runs the race-track. To our right at the end of the oval are the twelve stalls from which the chariots will break. The rest of the oval is surrounded by tier on tier of marble seats, crowded with at least 250,000 spectators in the most festive of holiday moods.

Such is the setting which we must re-create. But no words will describe the scene when the signal cloth is dropped and the chariots, each pulled by four plunging, galloping horses, burst forth. On the race-track anything goes and there are no fouls. Seven times for a distance of almost three miles those chariots careen around the track. As each lap is finished, one egg is taken down and one dolphin turned. On the track, as the last turn is made, one chariot may collide with another and the eight horses will at once be piled up in a struggling, squealing mass with one

RELIEFS FROM AN ARCH OF THE AGE OF MARCUS AURELIUS: GRANTING MERCY TO BARBARIANS: SACRIFICING BEFORE TEMPLE OF JUPITER CAPITOLINUS
PALAZZO DEI CONSERVATORI, ROME
161-180 A.D.

charioteer flung clear and another under the horses' hooves. The rest will dash for the chalk-mark which is the winning line. The 250,000 people will be on their feet yelling and shrieking. They will fall quiet until the winning colour is announced, then there will be a cheer for the winner, bets will be paid, and the crowd will settle back to wait for the next race.

There were three-horse, two-horse and one-horse races. There were races where a man handled three to four horses, jumping from the back of one to the back of another. There were rope-dancers, acrobats, foot races, performing bears, horses that counted, and the four-horse chariot races. There was not only the colour and the excitement and the chance, as the poet Ovid points out, of picking up a pretty girl—there was also the betting.

In Rome, the bet was on the colour. Except for a short period there were four stables only—the Whites, Blues, Greens, and Reds. A fantastic number of people were engaged in the breeding, training, and care of the four stables. Winning charioteers were mentioned in the Daily News Bulletin of Rome, which was posted each day in the Forum. Great charioteers became the toast of Rome. Diocles, the Spaniard, for example, won 1,462 victories in 4,257 races and in 150 A.D. retired after receiving $1,800,000 in prizes.

Winning gladiators were equally popular. In Rome the great centre for the gladiatorial games of the amphitheatre was the Colosseum which accommodated 50,000 spectators. But the popularity of the gladiatorial shows reached out everywhere, as the amphitheatres from Scotland to Antioch prove, except that in Greece there was a strong resistance to them. Nor were all gladiators condemned criminals or prisoners-of-war. Many a man took up the profession, as pugilists or matadors do today, for the money and the glory in it. In Pompeii, an inscription tells us that Celadus was the 'glory' and 'sigh' of the girls, and other inscriptions prove the fortunes made by successful gladiators. 'How many idle men,' says the Christian writer, Tertullian, 'contract themselves out to the sword, for love of combat.'

The games of the amphitheatre may, in a brief sketch of them, be divided into beast-hunts, sea-fights, and gladiatorial shows. The most spectacular of the sea-fights was presented by the Emperor Claudius in 52 A.D. on the Fucine Lake near Rome between a Sicilian and a Rhodian fleet with 19,000 men in all on board. Tens of thousands of spectators sat around the lake on the banks and hills. Claudius presided in a general's mantle and the signal to engage was given on a trumpet by a silver Triton

COLOSSEUM, ROME
ROMAN. C. 75—82 A.D. AND LATER

INTERIOR. COLOSSEUM, ROME
ROMAN. MAIN STRUCTURE c. 70—82 A.D.

POLLICE VERSO
GÉRÔME. 1824—1904

diving up from the water. Then the two fleets crashed together
in a desperate battle until the lake was a tangle of shattered warships and dead and dying men. Our rugby and even our bull-
fighting are rather tame by comparison.

This sort of thing was also presented in the Colosseum which
could be flooded and turned into a lake. The arena of the
Colosseum was often decked out, too, with bushes and rocks for
the beast-hunts. Sometimes, two beasts such as a rhinoceros and
an elephant were set to fight each other. At the games of
Septimius Severus in 202 A.D. the arena was transformed into a
ship which suddenly broke apart to show bears, lions, panthers,
ostriches, and bisons which at once attacked each other. In the
games of Nero the ground opened and a wood with fountains
and wild beasts sprang into view. On other occasions beasts were
let loose on unarmed criminals; or else the criminals were armed
and the populace watched their frantic efforts against lions and

tigers. The usual show, however, was a true beast-hunt with skilled hunters massacring camels, crocodiles, elephants, rhinoceri, hippopotami, lions, and the like. In his games, for example, the Emperor Trajan had 11,000 wild animals killed.

One corollary of this kind of spectacle was a tremendous organization both to capture the wild beasts and to bring them to Rome. Another was the elimination of tigers, lions, bears, and other wild animals from the Roman empire. Beasts had to be brought in from the forests of Germany or from the far reaches of Africa and Asia.

The culminating spectator sport was, of course, the gladiatorial contest. Every attempt was made to vary the exhibition—both in types of equipment used and in types of combat. You will see in museums fragments of the splendid armour used. Julius Caesar exhibited three hundred pairs of gladiators dressed in silver armour. Augustus gave eight shows in which, in all, 10,000 gladiators fought. Trajan used 10,000 in his spectacle, but that spectacle lasted, as has been mentioned, for 123 days.

The cost of the spectacles can scarcely be computed. In the early empire one city in Campania spent $20,000 on a three-day gladiatorial show. But in Rome alone, in 51 A.D., apart from shows put on by private individuals and officials, the games cost the treasury over eighty-five millions of dollars. Such was the price for amusing the Roman people.

The Roman games, the excesses of Roman luxury, and the canker of people on the dole are the natural products of a civilization which, unlike that of Periclean Athens, valued money and possessions above the achievements of the mind and the spirit. These phenomena were also signposts toward the collapse which was to overtake the Roman world. But in the first two centuries of the empire few people realized that Roman civilization was already rotting from within.

PHOTO. ALINARI

ARCH OF CONSTANTINE, ROME 315 A.D.

WHY ROME FELL

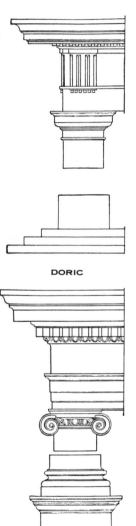

DORIC

IONIC

'IF,' WRITES GIBBON in his *Decline and Fall of the Roman Empire,* 'a man were called upon to fix the period in the history of the world when the condition of the human race was most happy and prosperous, he would, without hesitation, name that which elapsed from the death of Domitian to the accession of Commodus'—that is, the period from 98 to 180 A.D.

Yet in the next century the Roman empire crumbled. There were civil wars between 180 and 285 A.D. Of twenty-seven emperors or would-be emperors all but two met violent deaths. Meanwhile, the Persians raided to Antioch in the East and in Europe the barbarians broke through the frontiers. Huge tracts of country were devastated. The middle-class was squeezed out of existence. Farmers and labourers were transformed into serfs. When in 285 A.D. Diocletian pulled the empire together again, there was but little left of the prosperity of the *Pax Romana.*

It seems clear, then, that the causes of the collapse must, like hidden cancers, have been developing during Gibbon's period of happiness and prosperity, and some of the symptoms, at least, can be recognized. To take one example, in the first century of the empire there had still been a vigorous literature. But in the second century A.D. from Hadrian onward, apart from Suetonius' *Biographies of the Emperors,* the *Metamorphoses* of Apuleius, and the *Attic Nights* of Aulus Gellius, Latin literature is overcome by a sort of indolent apathy.

The same apathy began to exhibit itself in municipal life. In the first century wealthy men had gladly assumed the heavy financial burdens which were imposed on the local magistrates and senators. By the second century many cities had spent themselves into debt. There was the cost of repairing and main-taining the temples, public baths, and the like. There were also heavy expenditures for civic sacrifices, religious processions, feasts, and for the games necessary to amuse the proletariat.

The wealthy citizens of the municipalities who were, in effect, the middle-class, began to grow weary of the load; especially since the constantly rising taxation rates were shearing them closer and closer. Furthermore, they were expected to help their communities out of debt by 'voluntary' loans.

By the middle of the second century, there were cases where

compulsion had to be used to fill the local magistracies. There were other cases, beginning with Hadrian, where, when municipalities got into financial difficulties, imperial curators were put in charge and the cities lost their independence. The people did not seem to mind. As often happens today, they were quite willing to resign their control of affairs and to let the government take care of them.

This extension of paternalism was accompanied by a tremendous increase in the personnel of the imperial civil service. Each bureau expanded its field and new bureaux were constantly being created. By the time of Antoninus Pius, who ruled from 138 to 161 A.D., the Roman bureaucracy was as all-embracing as that of modern times. Naturally, too, as benevolent paternalism and bureaucracy took over, personal freedom tended to disappear. By the third century, to quote the historian Trever, 'the relentless system of taxation, requisition, and compulsory labour was administered by an army of military bureaucrats. . . . Everywhere . . . were the ubiquitous personal agents of the emperors to spy out any remotest case of attempted strikes or evasion of taxes. . . .'

To the cost of the bureaucracy was added the expense of the dole. Originally, this was passed out once a month. By the time of Marcus Aurelius, there was a daily distribution of pork, oil, and bread to the proletariat. Meanwhile, the expenditure on the public spectacles kept mounting. A hundred million dollars a year in Rome alone is a moderate estimate of what was poured out on the games. There was likewise an attempt to combine a subsidy to Italian farmers with charity to needy children. This was called the *alimenta* and was instituted by Nerva, who reigned from 96 to 98 A.D. His system was to lend money at five per cent instead of twelve per cent to farmers with the proviso that the interest should be used to support needy children. Boys received seventy cents a day, girls sixty.

And then there was the army. The army was essential to the security of the empire. The cost of it, though, more than doubled between 96 and 180 A.D.

All these expenditures had to be recovered from the taxpayer. To compound the difficulties, there was an adverse balance of trade. Roman currency, for example, poured into India and the East to pay for luxuries. Even in the time of Nero, Seneca estimated that it cost Rome five million dollars a year to import its luxuries from the East. In a word, though seemingly prosperous, in the second century A.D. the Roman empire was overspending to such an extent that it was moving to an economic

THE ROMAN ORDERS

CORINTHIAN

COMPOSITE

crisis. When in 167 A.D. Marcus Aurelius was faced by the attack of the Germanic Marcomanni and Quadi, he was forced to sell, as it were, the crown jewels as well as the household furnishings of his palace to finance the war. To add to his troubles a plague, brought back from the East, was ravaging the empire. By 180 A.D. at least one-fourth of the population of the whole empire, both civilian and military, had perished. In any estimate of the reasons for the decline of Rome, the moral and physical effects of this plague and the later one of 252-267 A.D. ought not to be omitted.

Marcus Aurelius also depreciated the currency by twenty-five per cent. For, as another symptom of the coming crisis, there was a creeping inflation. It has been asserted in modern times that the dollar is worth only fifty cents. If one recalls the prices of pre-First-World-War days, when a good average meal could be bought for a quarter, the dollar has depreciated more than that. The Roman *denarius* went further. In the reign of Augustus it was worth twenty cents. By the time of Diocletian it was stabilized at about two cents.

Thus, the seemingly happy world of Gibbon's day was sleep-walking its way to catastrophe. The plague contributed to the decline. But, even before the plague, the Roman world was rotting from within. Government paternalism, bureaucracy, inflation, an ever-increasing taste for the brutal and brutalizing spectacles of the amphitheatre and the circus were symptoms of a spiritual malaise which had begun when political freedom was tossed away in the interests of peace, security, and materialism. There was the canker of slavery and the equally dangerous practice of keeping a segment of the population permanently on the dole. There was free labour subsisting on starvation wages because of the competition of slavery. At the other end of the scale lolled a group of multi-millionaires for whom no luxury was too extravagant. Nor did anyone perceive that inflation and rising taxation must ultimately squeeze the middle-class out of being. Meanwhile, a tide of Oriental religions tried to fill the spiritual vacuum. A sense of futility seemed to permeate society. There were many outstanding administrators and good governors but, on the whole, the Roman spirit which had conquered the world seemed to have dissolved into an indolence which preferred ease and comfort to a facing up to the dangers which threatened civilization.

Some authors suggest that the change in racial stock was responsible for this attitude. Others mention the plague and malaria as possible causes. One might better, perhaps, simply call it the disease of materialism or, if you like, of the 'affluent society'. In any case, few Romans or Italians now served in the legions. Beginning with Hadrian, the army was decentralized, immobilized, and, if one may invent a word, foreignized. It was Hadrian who built the great wall in Britain from the Tyne to the Solway. He also constructed a three-hundred-and-forty-mile-long palisade of split oak logs, nine feet high, along the frontier in Germany and Raetia. Behind this palisade were forts of earthworks which his successor replaced with stone.

Behind this Maginot Line, if one may be permitted an anachronism, and elsewhere in the empire, each legion was settled in a permanent camp. This camp often became a town such as Lambaesis in Africa or Carnutum in Austria. Moreover, Hadrian also began the policy of filling up the army with provincials from the area to be defended and of allowing the Germans to settle in the Danubian provinces, provided they served in the auxiliary troops when called upon. Thus by the time of Marcus Aurelius the army was composed either of ignorant countrymen from the most backward parts of the empire or of foreigners. In spirit and in culture they were peasant wolves with little, if any,

UNIVERSITY PRINTS, BOSTON

PONT DU GARD. NÎMES, FRANCE
ROMAN. C. 16 B.C. OR I CENT. A.D.

respect for the fat sheep they were supposed to protect. This divorce between barbarized army and civilized but soft civilians was the immediate cause of the collapse.

The apathetic Romans soon reaped the whirlwind they had sown. When in 193 A.D. Commodus, the brutal son of the Stoic emperor, Marcus Aurelius, was assassinated, a man named Pertinax put on the purple. He promised large gifts to the legions and to the praetorians, those soldiers who from their camp just outside Rome dominated the city. When he tried to enforce discipline, he in turn was murdered. The praetorians then sold the throne to Didius Julianus for a bribe of $1,250 per soldier. But the legions promptly put forward three other candidates. After three years of civil war Septimius Severus emerged as the victor. He ruled harshly but capably until 211 A.D. and had the good luck to die in bed in Britain. You can see his triumphal arch today in the Roman Forum.

But the army now knew its power. During the next twenty-four years, four Caesars ruled and four Caesars were assassinated. Then in 235 A.D., the legions raised the first 'barbarian' to the purple. This man, Maximinus, was a Thracian peasant of mixed Gothic and Alan descent who had begun his career as a common soldier. According to the legends about him, he was eight-and-a-half feet tall, could crumble stones in his hands and break a horse's leg with a kick of his heel, and each day ate forty pounds of meat and drank nearly eight gallons of wine.

UNKNOWN ROMAN:
TERRA COTTA BUST
MUSEUM OF FINE ARTS,
BOSTON
1ST C. B.C.

Maximinus never even visited Rome. His three years of rule were a reign of terror. After him followed fifty years of military anarchy. During that half-century twenty-six Caesars in all donned the purple and only one died peacefully in bed. Almost all of them were first the nominees and then the victims of the soldiers. In one year, 259 A.D., there were eighteen pretenders to the throne. Sections of the empire seceded, as, for example, Gaul, in which Postumus, and after him Albinus, held power for fifteen years with Britain and Spain as tributary provinces.

As if the civil wars were not enough to fill full the cup of woe, in the East the second Persian empire, which had replaced the Parthians in the Middle East, raided as far as Antioch and took the Emperor Valerian prisoner. At the same time the caravan city, Palmyra, rose to power under Odenathus and his widow, the beautiful and ambitious Zenobia. From 267 A.D. until her defeat by Aurelian in 272 Zenobia controlled the whole Near East, except for parts of Asia Minor and Alexandria in Egypt.

ARCH OF SEPTIMIUS SEVERUS, FORUM, ROME
ROMAN.   203 A.D.

The situation in Europe was even worse. Here, the Germans burst through the barrier of the Rhine and the Danube. In 257 A.D. the Goths overran Dacia, crossed the Danube, and penetrated into Greece. In 267 another tribe, the Heruli, sacked Athens. In 269 the Heruli and the Goths, in their biggest invasion, crossed the Danube with their families, 320,000 strong, and sailed with 2,000 ships into the Mediterranean. Fortunately for Rome the Emperor Claudius cut to pieces both their fleet and their army.

Further west another German tribe, the Marcomanni, had already in 254 penetrated Italy as far as Ravenna. A few years later the Alamanni got as far as Milan. Meanwhile, in 256 and 258, the Franks and allied tribes swept across the Rhine and ravaged the whole country as far as Tarragona in Spain. Still farther west the Saxons were sailing against Britain. To pile disaster on destruction, from about 252 A.D. the second plague, which has already been mentioned, devastated the Roman world for fifteen years. Alexandria lost two-thirds of its population and in Rome, at the peak of it, five thousand died each day.

The Emperor Aurelian did something to check the complete

A GAUL KILLING HIMSELF AND HIS WIFE
TERME, ROME

ABOUT 240—200 B.C., ROMAN COPY

disintegration of the empire. In addition to capturing Zenobia, he brought back Gaul, Britain, and Spain into the empire. But it was he who abandoned Dacia and built around Rome the great wall, twelve feet thick and twenty high, of which you can still see large sections in the imperial city. But Aurelian was assassinated, and so there was another period of chaos until in 285 A.D. the Illyrian, Diocletian, gained control.

Such is a brief sketch of the ordeal through which the Roman world passed in the one hundred and five years from the death of Marcus Aurelius to the accession of Diocletian. Mere words can scarcely convey the agony through which the inhabitants of that world passed. There was murder, rape, and pillage. What the soldiers or the barbarians spared, the agents of the emperors took for taxes. The old bureaucracy of senators and knights was pretty well exterminated. In its place came a military hegemony of soldiers who had risen from the ranks. Both the army which now included many barbarians, and the senate were equalitarianized and, in consequence, barbarized. It was the members of the military who formed the new landed aristocracy. The middle-class and labour had both become serfs of the state. Increasing taxation and paternalism meant, inevitably, regimentation.

Such was the situation when in 285 A.D. Diocletian took charge. He drove back the barbarians and reconstituted the empire. But it was a new type of Roman empire, one which was ruled by an Oriental despotism. No one could approach Diocletian without prostrating himself on the ground and kissing the hem of his garment. Furthermore, he appointed three other Caesars and divided the empire into four prefectures. His own capital was not at Rome but at Nicomedia in Asia Minor. The army was reformed and enlarged; and was composed chiefly of Germans and Sarmatians or else of the sons of veterans. A mobile force of infantry was supplemented by a powerful cavalry. For the foot-soldiers of the legions could no longer be trained in the old Roman way.

In the old Roman fashion, however, Diocletian went in for colossal buildings, such as his enormous baths in Rome. But his other civil measures illustrated what had happened to the peace and prosperity of scarcely more than a century before. To cure inflation he devalued the silver *denarius*. This was a devaluation, in all, of 97.8 per cent. Then, in 301 A.D., Diocletian issued an edict fixing the maximum prices for all goods and the wages of all labour. To cite a few examples only, ham was priced at twenty cents a pound, butter at sixteen cents, and eggs at nine cents a dozen. Wheat, however, brought $1.25 a bushel. Unskilled labour was paid eighteen cents a day and bricklayers thirty-six cents.

Death was the penalty for breaking the code. But prices continued to rise. Meanwhile, so complete had been the breakdown that taxes were now often being paid in kind, that is, not in money but in actual grain, sheep, cattle, and the like. To collect the taxes, the local senatorial class in each municipality was made responsible—that is, these men, who were the middle-class of the Roman world, were given each year a fixed sum to raise. What they failed to collect from their fellows, they had to put up from their own purses. This would be as if the federal government of Canada assigned a fixed amount of taxes to, for example, the city of Toronto and made a thousand men responsible for gathering the whole amount.

This local senatorial class was now made up of all who owned fifteen acres or their equivalent. They had to serve as tax-collectors without pay. If they attempted to enlist in the army or to join the clergy to avoid their duties, they were forced to return to their jobs. Finally, they were forbidden to change their residences or to dispose of their own property without permission. For, somehow, the crushing cost of the army and of a top-heavy bureaucracy had to be met. Thus, the middle-class was taxed out of existence.

The same principle of regimentation was imposed on farmers and on free labour. Farmers were tied to the soil and, by law, the son of a farmer had to become a farmer. Similarly, the son of a baker or of a metal-worker or of a dock-worker each had to follow the profession of his father. Furthermore, all artisans, traders, shop-owners and the like had to furnish each year to their city and to the state a specified amount of their products at a price fixed by the state.

There was no escape from this relentless regimentation. For regimentation was the end-result of the abdication of political freedom and of the pursuit of materialism. The welfare state had become a despotism.

This new and dreary type of empire still possessed sufficient power to hold the frontiers against the barbarians for another century. In 324 A.D. Constantine the Great won the purple under the sign of the Cross. Hence came an edict of toleration for Christianity.

But the despotism was tightened rather than eased; and it is an interesting note on the morals of the age that within three years of his championship of orthodox Christianity at the Council

PHOTO. HIRMER

COLOSSAL HEAD OF CONSTANTINE THE GREAT
PALAZZO DEI CONSERVATORI, ROME

ABOUT 315—330 A.D.

of Nicaea, Constantine put a nephew to death, drowned his wife in a bath, and murdered a son.

Constantine placed his capital at Byzantium, which he renamed Constantinople. Thus Rome was now no longer the centre of the empire. Finally, in 395 A.D., the former Roman world was formally divided into an Empire of the East and an Empire of the West.

The eastern empire survived until the capture of Constantinople by the Turks in 1453 A.D. In the west, Visigoths, Ostrogoths, Vandals, Franks, and Huns burst over the frontiers and the Jutes, Angles, and Saxons planted themselves in Britain. In 410 A.D. Alaric and his Goths sacked Rome. Then, in 476 A.D., the last of the Caesars, Romulus Augustulus, was dethroned. The Germanic kingdoms took the place of the *Imperium Romanum.*

Yet the idea of the empire did not die. For that matter no one was conscious of any break with the past. It had taken almost three centuries for the unity of the *Pax Romana* to be transformed to the kingdoms of the Goths, the Franks, the Lombards, and the rest, and these kingdoms, especially in Italy and France, believed themselves to be carrying on the Roman tradition. With Charlemagne and his successors the idea of the universal Roman empire was revived; and it haunted Europe for centuries.

The major point is that there was no neat slicing off the periods, as it were with a knife, so that one segment was in people's minds labelled the period of the Roman empire and the other, the Dark Ages. Above all, the empire left behind it a great inheritor, the Christian Church. Through it, more than by any other single agency, a spark of culture was kept alive. It was because of the gradualism of its fall that the Roman empire put an ineffaceable imprint on Europe and, through it, on the New World.

What, then, are a few of the ways in which Rome still influences us today? There is, first of all, language. As you know, all the Romance languages are descended from Latin; and no educated Anglo-Saxon can, as in this very sentence I am writing, speak or write anything but the most elementary of sentences without using words derived from Latin. Nor is it any accident that the very forms of our letters are Roman.

Architecture is a word derived from Greek. But triumphal arches and columns such as the Arc de Triomphe or Nelson's Column in Trafalgar Square are Roman. Beyond that somewhat minor contribution, the Romans gave us the arch, the vault, and the dome. Their inspiration is evident in St. Peter's of Rome and St. Paul's of London. They also built for permanence. Roman roads and Roman concrete are like the best of the Romans—solid, efficient, and enduring. In sculpture, except for portrait busts and their sculpture of animals, the Romans were inferior to the Greeks. In literature, in spite of writers such as Virgil and Cicero, they must again yield the palm. But in law they took over the 'natural law' of the Stoics and made it into the *ius gentium,* the law of nations. They are, in fact, the originators of law as we know it, though their actual codes have had their chief influence on Latin nations.

Their greatest achievement, perhaps, was in their ability to rule an empire with even-handed justice and, gradually, to infuse a sense of unity through the whole. Like the British, the Romans allowed each segment of their empire its own peculiar customs but, little by little, drew them into the Roman way. Order, discipline, efficient administration—these were some of the qualities which Rome passed on to Western civilization.

As has often been said, if everything that stands in the world is Roman, everything that moves is Greek. The Romans themselves might and did, in general, like modern North Americans, prefer the rhetorical, the sentimental, the colossal, the magnificent, and the over-decorated. Yet in their best days, they were able to recognize in Greek art, literature, and philosophy, 'the light that never was on sea or land'. Thus, they passed on to us something of that Greek spirit which is the wine of the mind and the imagination. During the Renaissance that Greek spirit once more revived Europe. Out of that quickening emerged what is best in modern civilization.

CENTAURS BY ARISTEAS AND PAPIAS CAPITOLINE MUSEUM, ROME 2ND C. A.D.

In this book I have attempted to sketch something of the history, life, and ideas of the Greek and Roman world. Much, of necessity, has been omitted.

I have also tried to indicate what we of today owe to our classical heritage. Each generation is inclined to think that its discoveries and its way of life are unique. This is particularly true, perhaps, of the present. As a result, the study of Greek and Latin and of the classical civilizations is very much out of fashion. Yet it was Sir Winston Churchill who once said: 'He who can look furthest into the past, can see furthest into the future.'

For whether we like it or not, the past of Greece and Rome lives on in us. If we are wise, we of the present will use the study of Greece and Rome both as a corrective for modern trends and as an inspiration for achievement.

CHRONOLOGY

PERIODS OF GREEK HISTORY (all dates B.C.)

The Minoan-Mycenean Civilization and the World of Homer (2400–800)

c.2400	Bronze Age in Crete. Minoan civilization begins.
c.1400	End of Minoan dominance of the Aegean.
1400–1200	The Mycenean "Empire" of the Achaeans.
1200–1100	Dorian migrations. Iron Age begins.
c.850–800	Homer. The *Iliad* and the *Odyssey* begin European literature.

The Formative Age of Greece (800–500)

776	First Olympic Games.
c.750	Hesiod's didactic epic, *Works and Days*.
750–550	Greek colonization and trade. Monarchy gives way to aristocracy (800-700). Coinage is introduced (700-600). Age of Tyrants (650-550). Era of elegiac, iambic, and lyric poetry. Early development of sculpture, architecture, philosophy, science, and prose writing.
700–550	Rise of Sparta.
612	Capture of Nineveh. End of Assyrian Empire.
594	Solon archon in Athens. First steps toward democracy.
560–514	Tyranny of Peisistratids in Athens.
550–529	Cyrus the Great founds the Persian Empire. He takes over Lydia and the Greek cities of Asia Minor.
508	Cleisthenes sets up democracy in Athens.

The Persian Wars (499–479)

499–494	Revolt of Greeks of Asia Minor. Athens and Eretria send help.
492	First Persian Expedition wrecked off Mt. Athos.
490	Marathon.
480	Thermopylae and Salamis. The Western Greeks defeat the Carthaginians at Himera.
479	Plataea and Mycale. End of Persian menace.

The Great Age of Athens (478–404)

Cultural outburst, centring in Athens. The three great names in sculpture are Myron, Pheidias, and Polycleitus. The Parthenon (dedicated in 438) is the supreme achievement in architecture. In tragedy, Aeschylus (525-456), Sophocles (c. 496-406), and Euripides (c. 480-406) are the premier poets; in comedy, Aristophanes (c. 448-385). Herodotus (c. 484-425), and Thucydides (c. 471-400) write history. Socrates (c. 470-399) is one of many philosophers.

Meanwhile, from 477 to 440 Athens establishes a naval and trade empire in the Aegean and Black Sea areas. Her red-figured vases capture the pottery trade of the Mediterranean.

460–429   Pericles leads the Athenian democracy.
431–404   The Peloponnesian War. Athens is defeated and her "Great Age" ends.

The Fourth Century

Politically and economically, Greece is in chaos. Literature and sculpture (Scopas, Praxiteles, and Lysippus) still maintain high standards. In philosophy this is the century of Plato and Aristotle.

404–371   Spartan supremacy.
401   March of the Ten Thousand (described in Xenophon's Anabasis).
399   Trial and execution of Socrates for impiety.
c.387   Plato founds his "Academy" in Athens.
371–362   Theban supremacy (Epaminondas and Pelopidas).
338   Battle of Chaeroneia. Philip II of Macedon takes over Greece.
342–291   Menander of Athens, great poet of "The New Comedy."
c.335   Aristotle founds his school in the Lyceum at Athens.
334–326   Alexander the Great conquers the Persian Empire.
323   Death of Alexander.

The Hellenistic World (323–30)

In this era the nation-states of Macedonia, Syria, Egypt, ruled by Macedonians and Greeks, come to the fore. There are two federal Greek leagues, the Achaean and Aetolian. Rhodes is important. In Asia Minor the kingdom of Pergamum is founded by Attalus I in 241. In this same second century, the Parthians, later to be rivals of the Romans, occupy Mesopotamia.

This period is the period of Graeco-Oriental culture, called Hellenistic. Sculpture is realistic and emotional. Literature is "modern." It is also the epoch of science, of state-socialism, and credit-capitalism.

Rome swallowed this Hellenistic world. Significant dates

here are the Battle of Pydna (168), the annexation of Syria (63), and the annexation of Egypt (30).

PERIODS OF ROMAN HISTORY
(all dates B.C. until the reign of Augustus)

The Kingdom and the Republic to the Gracchi (753–133)

c.800   Etruscans land in Italy. They establish a hegemony from Milan almost to Naples.

753   Traditional date of the founding of Rome.

509   Founding of the Roman Republic.

390   Rome sacked by the Gauls.

343–290   The Samnite Wars. Rome dominant in Italy.

287   *Lex Hortensia* ends struggle between Patricians and Plebeians.

272   Capture of Tarentum. Rome mistress of Italy south of the Po. Greek influence pours into the city.

264–241   First Punic War. Rome acquires her first provinces.

218–201   Second Punic War. Rome rules Western Mediterranean.

200–133   Rome takes over the Near East. The plunder from her successful wars has produced a "society of beggars and millionaires." Meanwhile Graeco-Roman literature has begun with authors such as Plautus, Terence, and Ennius.

The Collapse of the Republic (133–27)

133–121   Two nobles, Tiberius and Gaius Gracchus, attempt to break the "Rule of the Senate" and to reform the economic evils of Italy. Both are assassinated by the *Optimates* (The Best People), but they have founded the *Populares* (People's Party).

102–100   Marius founds a professional army which will follow its general against the State.

90–88   Revolt of the Italians. Civil War.

87–83   The Marian massacres and the dictatorship of the *Populares*. Meanwhile Sulla, the Optimates' general, defeats Mithradates of Pontus in the first Mithradatic war (89-85).

83   Return of Sulla. Civil War. Sulla dictator until 79, dies in 78.

74–63   Third Mithradatic War.

73–71   Slave revolt, led by Spartacus, in Italy.

70   Crassus and Pompey consuls. Cicero prosecutes a corrupt governor of Sicily, Verres, and becomes a political force.

67   Pompey defeats the pirates.

66–62   Pompey overcomes Mithradates and overruns the Near East, except for Egypt.

63   Cicero, as consul, crushes the Catilinian Conspiracy.

60   Formation of First Triumvirate of Pompey, Crassus, and Caesar.

58–52   Caesar conquers Gaul.

53   Crassus is killed by Parthians at Battle of Carrhae.

49–45   Civil War. Caesar defeats Pompey at Pharsalus (48) and Cato at Thapsus (46).

44   Assassination of Caesar.

43   Second Triumvirate of Octavian (Augustus), Antony, and Lepidus. Cicero is proscribed and murdered. Brutus and Cassius are defeated at Philippi (42).

31   Battle of Actium. Octavian defeats Antony and Cleopatra.

27   The Principate of Augustus (Octavian) begins.
        Note: c. 70-43 is the Ciceronian period of letters with authors such as Lucretius, Cicero, Catullus, and Caesar. Then comes the Augustan age in which Virgil, Horace, Tibullus, Propertius, and Ovid are the outstanding poets, and Livy writes his history.

The Roman Empire from Augustus to Marcus Aurelius (27 B.C. to 180 A.D.) (All dates A.D.)

14   Death of Augustus.

14–68   The Julio-Claudians (Tiberius, 14-37; Caligula, 37-41; Claudius, 41-54; Nero, 54-68). In spite of the excesses of Caligula and Nero, the Roman world is in general well governed. Southern Britain is conquered under Claudius. In 60 Boadicea's revolt is crushed. The principal writers are Seneca, Lucan, and Petronius, of whose summarized novel, the *Satyricon*, the *Cena Trimalchionis* is the longest excerpt.

69–96   The Flavians (Vespasian, 69-79; Titus, 79-81; Domitian, 81-96). In 70 Jerusalem is captured and the Jews dispersed. In 79 an eruption of Vesuvius destroys Pompeii and Herculaneum. The "Silver Age" of Latin Literature (Pliny the Elder, Quintilian,

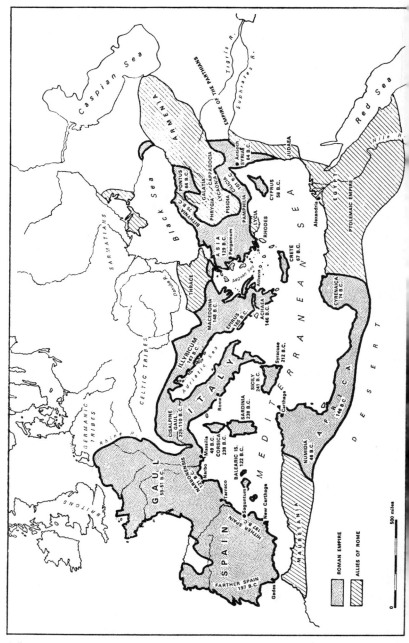

The Roman Empire at the End of the Republic

Martial, Tacitus, Juvenal, Pliny the Younger) begins and continues into the reign of Hadrian.

96–180 The Five Good Emperors (Nerva, 96-98; Trajan, 98-117; Hadrian, 117-138; Antoninius Pius, 138-161; Marcus Aurelius, 161-180). Roman Empire at its greatest extent. Era of peace and prosperity. 157-160, a plague decimates the Roman World. 165-175, Severe wars with the Germans.

The Ordeal of the Empire (180–395)

In this period the army makes and unmakes emperors. In the East the Second Persian Empire (Sassanids) replaces the Parthians as Rome's rival. Meanwhile the German tribes break the frontier and ravage Britain, Gaul, Spain, North Italy, and the Danubian provinces. As the Empire declines the Christian Church grows.

260 Second great plague at its height.
267 Germanic Heruli sack Athens.
270–275 Aurelian captures Zenobia of Palmyra and reconquers the Near East. He builds a wall around Rome.
285–305 Diocletian re-establishes the Empire with four capitals and four rulers. Last severe persecution of the Christians.
313 Constantine the Great issues Edict of Toleration for Christianity.
324–337 Constantine sole ruler. Founds Constantinople (330).
325 Council of Nicaea and Nicene Creed.
389–395 Theodosius the Great. Christianity the official religion. On his death the Empire is formally divided into eastern and western halves.

Fall of the Western Empire (395–476)

In this period Germanic Kingdoms are founded on the ruins of the Western Empire in Britain, Gaul, Spain, Africa, and Italy. Attila the Hun, also ravages the West.

410 Sack of Rome by the Goths under Alaric.
451 Attila defeated at the Battle of Chalons.
476 Deposition of Romulus Augustulus and end of the Western Roman Empire. The Eastern Empire (Byzantine) endures until the capture of Constantinople by the Turks (1453).

ADDITIONAL READING

Starr, Chester G., *History of the Ancient World*. New York, 1965.

Robinson, Charles A., *Ancient History* (2nd ed. revised by A. L. Boegehold). New York, 1967.

Trever, A. A., *History of Ancient Civilization* (2 vols.). New York, 1939.

Robinson, C. A., *Ancient History*. New York, 1951.

Forsdyke, Sir John, *Greece Before Homer*. London, 1957.

Ventris, Michael and John Chadwick, *Documents in Mycenean Greek*. Cambridge, 1956.

Webster, T. B. L., *From Mycenae to Homer*. London, 1958.

Roebuck, C., *Ionian Trade and Colonization*. New York, 1959.

Jones, A. H. M., *Athenian Democracy*. Oxford, 1957.

Livingstone, Sir Richard, *The Greek Genius* (2nd ed.). London, 1915.

Zimmern, Sir Alfred, *The Greek Commonwealth* (5th ed.). Oxford, 1931.

Gardiner, E. Norman, *Athletics of the Ancient World*. Oxford, 1930.

Quennell, Marjorie and C. H. B., *Everyday Things in Ancient Greece* (2nd ed.). London, 1954.

Fuller, B. A. G., *History of Greek Philosophy* (3 vols.). New York, 1932.

Lord Bertrand Russell, *Wisdom of the West* (pp. 10-121). New York, 1959.

Tarn, W. W., *Hellenistic Civilization* (3rd ed.). Toronto, 1952.

Hadas, Moses, *A History of Greek Literature*. New York, 1950.

Beazley, J. D. and B. Ashmole, *Greek Sculpture and Painting*. Cambridge, 1932.

Flickinger, R. C., *The Greek Theatre and its Drama* (4th ed.). Chicago, 1936.

Pallotino, Massimo, *Etruscan Painting*. Lausanne, 1952.

Cary, Max, *A History of Rome*. London, 1954.

Showerman, Grant, *Rome and the Romans*. New York, 1931.

Johnston, Mary, *Roman Life*. Chicago, 1957.

Abbott, F. F., *The Common People of Ancient Rome*. New York, 1911.

Louis, Paul, *Ancient Rome at Work* (translated from the French ed. of 1912 by E. B. F. Waring). New York, 1927.

Hadas, Moses, *Roman Literature*. New York, 1952.

Dill, Sir Samuel, *Roman Society from Nero to Marcus Aurelius*. New York, 1956.

Hamilton, E., *The Roman Way*. New York, 1932.

Mauri, A., *Pompeii* (5th ed.). Rome, 1948.

Mauri, A., *Roman Painting*. Lausanne, 1958.

Rostovtzeff, M. A., *Caravan Cities*. Oxford, 1932.

Glover, T. R., *Conflict of Religions in The Early Roman Empire* (9th ed.). London, 1930.

Gibbon, Edward, *The Decline and Fall of the Roman Empire* (condensed ed. by Dero. A. Saunders). New York, 1952.

Lot, F., *The End of the Ancient World and Beginning of the Middle Ages*. New York, 1931.

Livingstone, Sir Richard, ed., *The Legacy of Greece*. Toronto, 1928.

Bailey, C., ed., *The Legacy of Rome*. London, 1923.

Asimov, Isaac, *Greeks: A Great Adventure*. Boston, 1965.

Asimov, Isaac, *Roman Empire*. Boston, 1967.

White, Lynn, Jr., ed., *Transformation of the Roman World*. Berkeley, 1966.